Jesus Is Still Passing By

Secrets for a Victorious Life

study guide

J. Bennett Easterling

Copies of this book may also be purchased online at Amazon, Barnes and Noble, and other online retailers.

For information, contact
MSI Press
1760-F Airline Highway, #203
Hollister, CA 95023

Cover Photograph by Neil Anderson
Cover Design by Carl Leaver
Proofreading by Nora Dluzak & Linda Collier

Permissions gratefully received from George Abbott, Safaa Abramson, Roger Baldwin, Beacon Publishing, Jimmy Bennett, Alice Faye Brown, Joy Dawson, Justin Demalo, Richard Dluzak, Emily Durham, Dorothy Easterling, Kari Engen, Talisa Ernstmann, John and Susan Fitzgerald, Jentezen Franklin, John Guy, Fritz Habeman, Lois Harris, Rick Hunt, Robin Kam, Judy Matthews, Louis and Renee McGraw, Jackie Miller, Dale and Terry O'Shields, Our Daily Bread Ministries, John Paran, C. Vernon Vickers, Paul Yates, and George Zachriah.

Library of Congress Control Number 2019901404

ISBN: 9781933455815

DEDICATION

This book is dedicated to those convinced God's Word is true yet sometimes struggle to relate it to everyday lives. Don't give up! Your quest is a noble one. Remember, diamonds and gold must be mined from dirt and rocks. Ask Jesus to open your heart to all God has for you.

Contents

ACKNOWLEDGMENTS

I wish to acknowledge the following people who contributed to this book in their own ways:

- My beloved Dot. Our love is from heaven, God having personally set it to music long ago. Like the heavenly planets, our lives move in God's ordained orbit. Our love is secure in the knowledge that what He joined together shall never veer off-course. Some things are blissfully eternal.
- The late Elder Ira Easterling, my father, who showed us that humility and integrity pleases God, blesses others, and crowns a life with overflowing joy.
- Senior Pastor Dale O'Shields, who teaches that God's Word is so much more than theology—that it reveals real life principles we need every day. His vision and lifelong devotion to sharing the good news of the Messiah are truly inspirational.
- Neil Anderson for use of his photograph for the front cover.
- Nora Dluzak and Linda Collier for proofreading galleys and original manuscript.
- Publisher and friend Betty Leaver who brings out the best in her authors, giving a voice to many who would otherwise go unheard.
- Those who generously reviewed drafts of this manuscript and offered invaluable insights and suggestions. Jesus was

speaking of you in his Sermon on the Mount. Your kindness is deeply appreciated.

Finally, thanks are given to those of you who agreed to share your personal stories. God will be honored, and many will be encouraged to learn that Jesus is still passing by.

PREFACE

Do the miracles of Jesus have anything to say to you? How do they apply to your everyday life? And, are miracles still happening?

The Chicago Cubs baseball team in its glory days was a powerhouse, loved by its fans and feared by opponents. Then they lost their mojo for the next 108 years, becoming a laughing stock. People told and retold of the day in 1945 when the team's owner barred a billy goat from a World Series game, despite the owner having bought his "guest" a valid ticket. The goat's owner supposedly put a curse on the Cubs who never won another World Series.

Still, their die-hard fans stuck with them, dreaming that one day their beloved cellar-dwellers would throw off the so called "voodoo hex." Sure enough, in 2016 the Cubs exploded, again becoming an awesome force, clobbering opponents to win their division title. And, in a dramatic seventh game, they won their first World Series in more than a hundred years!

Tour Europe today, and you'll see some of the most magnificent edifices ever built by men. Stunning gold-gilded cathedrals display treasured works of art—all centered around God, his Son Jesus, holy people, and events of the Bible. Tourists are awestruck that the Christian faith inspired artists to such great feats.

Sadly, tourists who stick around to attend Sunday Mass or worship services in those incomparable cathedrals discover the crowds once filling them are long gone. Awesome in beauty, yes, but now reduced to empty shells.

Yet, a few die-hard dreamers will not give up. They slip in and out of skeletal services, yearning for Europe to be kindled anew—a new Holy

Ghost Pentecost sending the masses flowing back to God. They need a miracle.

The miracles of Jesus have a bit in common with the saga of the Chicago Cubs and the grand cathedrals of Europe. Few believed this low-born commoner was God Incarnate. Yet, when Christ walked the dusty Mediterranean roads telling people of God's love for them, his message was confirmed by miraculous signs.

The good news electrified towns and villages. Thousands trekked on long pilgrimages into dangerous places and remote countryside to see and hear the mystery man from Nazareth.

The Cubs may never win another World Series. The grand cathedrals of Europe may never again be filled with worshippers. And today, miracles find few believers. People consider themselves more sophisticated, highly educated, and scientifically oriented.

Maybe you're not a miracle skeptic, just a Doubting Thomas—not refusing to believe but asking for proof. That's reasonable enough, right?

Yet, to dismiss the signs God gave Jesus without exploring them would be foolhardy. Not only did they confirm he was the Son of God, but they harbor buried treasure: life lessons we still need—because human nature has not changed. Nor has God stopped talking to people. As Jesus, quoting Isaiah (54:13), said, we are all taught by God. Then he adds, "And those taught by God and who learn the truth from him will be attracted to me" (John 6:45). God speaks to us in many ways including his inspired word the Bible, the Holy Spirit, other people, our own life experiences, music—and miracles.

If you agree, let's get started relooking the miracles, inviting the Teacher to reveal to us his timeless secrets for a victorious life, and examining how the miracles of Jesus appear to us in the 21st century.

WATER INTO WINE
His First Miracle

(Gospel account in John 2:1-12)

Jesus was invited to a wedding along with his mother Mary. They accepted the invitation and went to share that special day with their friends.

A wedding was the greatest day in the life of a young Jewish girl. Her family and friends plus the groom, his family, and their friends went all out to give her a lavish celebration.

Our Lord was a lover of people. Jesus, his mother Mary, and the disciples were there to honor the wedding party and join them in celebrating their big day. What a great opportunity this gave Jesus to show them his love, to honor these simple folk, and share in their joy!

During the festivities, the wedding hosts ran out of wine. They may have underestimated the number of guests or couldn't afford to buy more—the Bible doesn't say. But, they were embarrassed.

Mary learned of their embarrassment and asked Jesus to help them. After some soul-searching because, as he told Mary, it was not time for him to begin his ministry yet, Jesus yielded to his mother's request and turned several containers of water into wine. Mary knew her son well—he would not ignore his own mother's request.

This miraculous sign at Cana was Jesus' first display of his glory. It convinced his disciples they had found their Messiah. Greater signs and wonders were soon to come.

Background

A word on the customs of the day may be illuminating: "There were many excellent vineyards in Palestine, and wine was made for common use. Water was scanty, especially at some seasons, and likely to be infected. Wine and milk were therefore the common beverages." (*Cruden's Complete Concordance*) Knowing this explains the important of having wine—beyond just its celebratory tradition.

In a tour of the Holy Land that my wife and I took a while back, our guides took us to Cana, still famous for this miracle. The fabled wines of Cana were being hawked by local merchants, eager to help tourists "savor" their experience.

Our friend John and I swallowed their bait hook, line and sinker. We purchased a sample and took it back to our hotel. That evening we opened it at dinner with great anticipation. Imagine our disappointment when it tasted like warm vinegar! Jesus must have been shaking his head and smiling.

Life Applications

Life Is To Celebrate

Nick's parents were uneducated Greeks, part of a vast horde of penniless immigrants who came to America searching for a better life.

His father scraped together enough money to buy a vending machine, then another one. A fledging livelihood was born.

Nick and his brother earned their college education by servicing those vending machines, refilling them with sandwiches, drinks, candy, and collecting the quarters and dollar bills. A hard scrapple existence.

Yet, when Nick's younger sister married, his parents rented an entire floor of the finest hotel in Mobile, Alabama for her wedding party, inviting hundreds of family and friends.

"Where did they get that kind of money?" I asked Nick.

"In our culture", he explained, "the moment a girl is born into the family, her parents begin saving for her wedding day. It's the most important day of her life—and theirs. And when her big day finally comes, their joy is unbounded. They feast and dance and celebrate all night long.

Most of us go through life assuming the "serious things" of life are the most important—but God intends us to enjoy life and celebrate the joys of others. Nick's parents had connected the dots.

For reflection:
Are you in love with people? (Jesus ranked it next to loving God.)
How do you show your love in practical ways?

Enjoy the Abundant Life

Some people seem to think God's only interest in us is to keep us out of hell and get us to heaven. Jesus wants to show us otherwise.

"I came that you might have life, enjoy it fully and abundantly, until it overflows." (John 10:10 paraphrased) Does that sound like Jesus is interested only in salvaging your soul?

Julie lights up a room simply by entering it. Her smile and good humor are infectious. Always joyful, jovial, and genuinely interested in what's going on with her friends. People gravitate to her, knowing they'll be greeted with a warm hug and welcoming smile. When they need someone to lean on, Julie is there to cheer them on.

Julie believes deeply in prayer so people share their heart burdens with her, knowing she will be lifting them up to God—and the next time she sees them she remembers to ask about the concerns they shared with her.

Julie has learned the secret of fruitful living, of loving God and others--of slipping past herself and launching out into the blessed life. She is the "dictionary definition" of a joyful Christian.

That's what Jesus wants for you. He longs for us to break free of narrow, mean, lonely, impoverished and selfish instincts and rise to live the abundant life.

For reflection:
What changes do you need to make to enjoy this abundant life?

Maintain Family Connections

Legendary coach Paul "Bear" Bryant could identify with Jesus. Considered by some to be the greatest college football coach ever, the Bear had already coached his name into history when he left Louisiana State University to go back home as Head Coach of his alma mater, the Crimson Tide of Alabama. LSU fans were astonished. "Why would you quit a championship team?" they demanded.

The Bear simply growled, "Momma called."

While Momma calling may reflect the relationship between Jesus and Mary, Coach Bryant's response is not really an example of a modern-day miracle, God is calling, and there are many examples of God calling.

Mother Teresa of India (now Saint Teresa of Calcutta) plucked thousands of starving and dying "untouchables" from the gutters of Calcutta—orphans, invalids, and elderly. She fed, clothed, sheltered, and medicated these hopeless ones, restored their lost dignity, saved their lives, showed them the love of Jesus, and told them he died to give them eternity. Mother Teresa modeled the heart, hands, and feet of Christ, giving her life to show them Christ's love. In time, Mother Teresa founded an order of nuns and created an endeavor that would live on after she passed on. But why did she begin doing this in the first place? God called.

Her biography contains letters she wrote to her confessor. In them, she relates the divine appearance that she experienced on a retreat and how that kept her going even when she no longer heard God's voice. That first miracle in her life created miracle after miracle in the lives of the poor of Calcutta and for those who followed in Mother Teresa's footsteps, the Missionaries of Charity [love].

For reflection:
How are you helping your family?
What could you do to make a difference to them?

THE WOMAN WHO TOUCHED JESUS

(Gospel account in Matthew 9:20-22; Mark 5:24-34; Luke 9:43-48)

A large crowd was following Jesus, pressing around him. A woman crept up quietly, trying to touch him. This dear lady had an internal bleeding disorder. For twelve years, she'd suffered under the care of many doctors and spent all her money to pay them. But, instead of getting better, she grew worse.

She'd heard of Jesus. So, she pressed through the crowd and slipped up behind him, thinking, "If I only touch his clothes, I'll be healed."

As soon as she touched his cloak, she felt the bleeding stop.

Background

This brave lady risked public humiliation by approaching Jesus unbidden. Women of her day were often not treated with dignity. She knew she would likely be ridiculed, but she was desperate enough to choose to face the consequences.

The disciples would not be sympathetic. They fancied themselves to be Jesus' palace guards, shooing the riffraff away, especially women and children. In their minds, Rabbi Jesus was too important to be distracted by the likes of this poor bleeding woman. Still, she had to try. What a heartwarming lesson! She risked disgrace to reach out and touch Jesus.

Really, in her mind, the choice was clear. After years of disappointments, of trying and failing, she realized doctors could not cure her. Yes, her doctors took away her money but not her chronic bleeding. If doctors couldn't help her, who could?

We don't know how she found out about Jesus. Maybe she witnessed one of his miracles, heard through word of mouth, or met an eye witness. In any case, she became convinced Jesus had been given a mysterious heaven-sent power. Her heart told her that he was the answer to her woes.

So, she pressed through the crowd, slipped up behind Jesus, and touched the edge of his cloak. Her bleeding stopped, completely and instantly. No more drugs, follow-up visits, doctors' bills, relapses, or embarrassing episodes. This precious lady was free at last!

Jesus asked, "Who touched me?" Everyone denied doing so. Peter pointed out the obvious, "Master, the people are pressing all around you." In other words, "How could we possibly know who it was?"

But Jesus said, "Someone touched me, for I knew it when power went out of me."

Jesus wasn't the only one who knew it. Something deep within this faith-filled lady told her God had healed her. The Spirit whispered blessed assurance. God confides deep secrets to believers, not revealed to others.

Her secret out, her cover blown, the trembling lady came and threw herself at Jesus' feet. She sensed the crowd's anger, knowing she'd violated all their highly valued traditions—a mere woman and worse yet, unclean, appealing to Jesus.

There in front of a horde of hostile, impatient, preoccupied self-seekers, she laid her heart bare. She told Jesus of her incurable bleeding, her years of pain. She confessed her desperation and her trust in his power to help her, hoping he would understand why she had touched him. She told him she felt her bleeding stop when she touched him. Then, she waited breathlessly for his response.

Instead of incurring his wrath, she heard these words of affirmation, "My daughter, your faith has made you well. Go in peace."

She might have avoided ridicule by slipping away quietly. However, from deep inside she summoned the courage to go public—to thank the Lord and give God the glory. By so doing, her story has inspired millions.

Clearly, God rewards those who seek him. This woman likely spent the rest of her life telling people of her personal encounter with the Savior who heals. God, bless his holy name, has equipped you to do the same. You're not a helpless weakling.

Life Applications

Faith in Action

Rosa Parks lived in Alabama at a time when segregation was the law of the land. Blacks were forced to drink from separate water fountains, use separate bathrooms, and attend separate schools and churches. Rosa knew it wasn't right, but what could one lone lady do against the law of the land? Yet, one fateful day, she couldn't take it anymore. She would not go silently into the gentle night. She took a middle seat on a city bus and refused to give up her seat and move to the back when a white person demanded it. Her brave act set off a powder keg of hatred, fear, and bigotry. She was arrested, insulted, reviled, and abused for refusing to play by the discriminatory rules of the day. Her bravery triggered the famous Montgomery Bus Boycotts where blacks were beaten and abused, but she had shined a bright light into one of America's darkest caves since slavery. People slowly began to realize the evils of forced segregation. Bloody civil rights marches followed, with participants getting killed. Yet, brave souls like Rosa Parks changed the world. Today, across America, streets, schools, and parks bear her name. School children studying the history of the civil rights struggle revere her and are inspired to demand their God-given rights of liberty and justice for all. Rosa paid a heavy price, but her courage changed our world.

James said it best, "Faith without action is dead." Rosa's faith was very much alive.

For reflection:
When have you overcome your fears and acted in faith?
How did that turn out?

Faith Under Fire

My father was a circuit riding minister in Mississippi during the Depression and World War II era. Since rural clergy were not paid a salary in those days, he supported his family of eight by farming 80 acres of black fertile land during the summers, plus trapping and selling the hides of furbearing animals in winter. Once, when a nearby land owner could not pay his taxes, Daddy was given an opportunity to add another 40-acres to his farm. Not being able to pay one's taxes was common during the Depression. So, Daddy went to the courthouse, paid the back taxes, and was given a Quit Claim Deed.

Years later, a neighbor looking through court records discovered that Daddy had neglected to convert his Quit Claim Deed to a regular deed. Seizing this opportunity, the scalawag falsified and signed an affidavit swearing the land was unclaimed, knowing Daddy had fenced it and was paying the taxes.

When Daddy told the tax assessor of the man's scheme, a court date was set to hear the case. On the day of the hearing, Daddy failed to show up. The swindling neighbor's lawyer convinced the judge to award the land to his client.

The man was a respected member of our community. One day he drove up to our house to make peace with Daddy. Mom refused to let him come inside the house so Daddy went out and sat in the man's car to talk. He claimed it was all a misunderstanding. Daddy knew better but let him have his say. When they parted, he even shook the scoundrel's hand. Mom was furious, but Daddy explained, "The Lord wants us to live in peace with our neighbors."

He believed that all vengeance belongs to God—and that God settles all accounts. And, the preacher slept well that night. (From the author's memoir, *Of God, Rattlesnakes and Okra, a preacher's boy tells his growing up story*, MSI Press.)

For reflection:
When has your faith been severely tested?
How would you describe your response?

The Power of Faith and Testimony

A friend worked for the US government, where separation of Church and State is strictly enforced. Her conditions of employment prohibited her from providing testimony, though her behavior served on many occasions as testimony.

One time, though, it seemed that God was asking her to show great courage, to take a more overt step, like the woman who touched Jesus did. She owned a little vial of holy water brought back from the baptismal site in the Jordan River, where she had once visited, and every time she looked at it, she saw the face of one of her employees. Finally, unable to resist, she summoned up the courage to do as God seemed to be directing her and took the holy water to her office.

She called the employee, a quiet man in his early thirties, whom she did not know well. When he came to her office, she said to him, "Please close the door because I'm not going to separate Church and State."

He closed the door, then sat down at the conference table in her office. She reached out and handed him the holy water, explained what it was, and told him about seeing his face whenever she looked at it.

He started crying. He told her that his daughter was just a few months old, in ICU, and on the verge of death. The holy water represented a sign of hope to him. (Oh, yes, the daughter lived; she is five years old this year.)

For reflection:
Have you ever felt intimidated when it came to providing testimony?
What did you do about it, and how did it turn out?
How can you prepare for the next opportunity?

JESUS HEALS A MAN BORN BLIND

(Gospel account in John 9:1-41)

As Jesus was walking along, he saw a man blind from birth. His disciples were principally interested in why misfortune had fallen on him—whose sin had caused it. Jesus addressed their questions, then healed the man.

"Teacher," his disciples asked, "why was this man born blind? Was it a result of his own sin or those of his parents?"

"It's not because of his sin or his parents' sin," Jesus answered. "He was born blind so the power of God could be seen (working) in him." Then, he added one more important piece of information, that it was important for him to work (show the power of God) now because night was coming (the time when he would be arrested and crucified and no longer able to work directly in this world as he could at that time).

Then Jesus spat on the ground, made mud with the spittle, and smoothed the mud over the blind man's eyes. "Go and wash your face in the Pool of Siloam," Jesus told him. So, the man went, washed his face, and came back seeing.

A little later, after the man had returned home, his neighbors could not accept what had happened, and they dragged the formerly blind man to the Pharisees. Upon seeing that the blind man could now see, the Pharisees refused to accept what their own eyes were telling them. Bamboozled is what we called it in the South when you have no clue what's happening. It had to be a trick Jesus was pulling on them! But the Pharisees had a problem: here was the man telling everyone who would listen, "Jesus did it."

So, they quizzed him again, "How did you receive back your sight?"

"He put some mud on my eyes; I washed my face, and now I can see."

Their interrogation was not going well, so they called in his parents. "Is this your son? You say that he was born blind; how is it that he can now see?"

His parents were afraid of the religious authorities, who had agreed that anyone saying they believed Jesus was the Messiah would be expelled from the synagogue. So, they gave an evasive answer.

"We know he is our son and that he was born blind. But we don't know how it is that he can now see, nor do we know who cured him. Ask him; he's old enough, and he can answer for himself!"

Still, the kangaroo court would not give up. To their delight, they discovered this healing took place on the Sabbath. So, they pronounced their verdict: "This fellow is not from God because he's working on the Sabbath."

Others said, "But how could an ordinary sinner do such miraculous signs?" So, there was a deep division of opinion among them.

His inquisitors called the man back for another round-robin session: "Give glory to God by telling the truth for we know this Jesus is a sinner."

"I don't know if he's a sinner." The man replied. "But I know this: I was blind, and now I can see!"

Still, they tried to prick holes in his story: "But what did he do? How did he heal you?"

"Look!" the man replied, "I told you once. Didn't you listen? Why do you want to hear it again? Do you want to become his disciples too?"

Then, they cursed him, and when they couldn't get him to denounce Jesus, they threw him out of the synagogue. When Jesus heard how shabbily they treated the man, he found him and asked, "Do you believe in the Son of Man?"

The man answered, "Who is he sir, because I would like to."

"You have seen him," Jesus told him," "and he is speaking to you!"

"Yes, Lord," the man said, "I believe!" And he worshipped Jesus.

Then Jesus told the new believer, "I have come into the world to give sight to the blind and to show those who think they see that they're blind."

"Is this the same fellow, that blind beggar?" People began asking. Some said yes. Some said "No, it can't be the same man, but it surely looks like him."

They asked him, and the beggar said, "I am the man." So, by his own word, this great miracle was confirmed.

Background

The disciples got it wrong again. When Jesus saw the blind man stumbling around, he set his heart on helping him. The disciples jumped to the conclusion it must be someone's fault.

It was commonly believed in those days that all sickness or misfortune is caused by sin. Many still harbor such suspicions, asking, "Why Lord? Why me God? Why him or her? What did I do to bring this on?"

Jesus was teaching us that people are not always the cause of their suffering. Someone needs to hear this. You may be blaming yourself for misfortune that's no fault of your own. Or, you may be asking the "why?" question of someone else's woes.

You've no doubt seen a loved one struggling—maybe a saintly grandparent, an innocent child, or kindly neighbor—and you've wondered why. Yet, it's not Christ-like to assume they've done something to deserve it. And, God forbid we try to figure out which of their sins caused it.

Jesus didn't say, "You're to blame for everything bad that happens to you." Instead, he said, "In this world you will have tribulation but be of good cheer. I have overcome the world." (John 16:33) Big difference!

Fault-finding is seldom the answer. Let's ask God to give us a tender heart—and show us how to help those in distress.

Follower of Jesus, let his compassion take hold in your heart. Pray for hurting people, try to help them if you can—but let's fight like a tiger against our lower victim-blaming instincts.

When Christ saw people suffering, his first instinct was compassion. Let's make it ours.

In the process, don't miss another spiritual principle of this story, exemplified by Jesus sending the man to wash his face. God often requires our participation. When we ask for God's help, he may ask us to partner with him. Cooperation opens the door to God's storehouse—and don't forget that Jesus said that the storehouse was to be filled now, not something planned for the future, because we do not know when it will be too late to work. His words about working while there is daylight is a call to action to work with him for the good of all.

Some things never change. Jesus is still a stumbling block. People are still divided today over the name and claims of Jesus. Is Jesus Son of the Living God? Is he the Messiah? Or was he a fraud, a charlatan wooing the masses with black magic miracles?

People were amazed. And why not? His family, neighbors, and everyone who knew him from childhood also knew he'd been born blind.

This is one of my favorite miracle stories—the blind man even had a sense of humor!

Life Applications

Compassion Comes First

Too often we play the blame game in the same way that the disciplines tried to blame the blind man—or his parents—for his blindness. This is a terrible response to suffering.

When Hurricane Katrina slammed into the Gulf Coast, killing more than 1,800 people and almost wiping New Orleans off the face of the earth, a friend told my wife, Dot, "Well, that's such a wicked place, the people had it coming."

To this Dot replied, "Well, we have two precious granddaughters living down there—and we don't think they're wicked."

"Oh, I didn't mean everybody!" she stammered. But finger-pointing is a popular sport.

For reflection:
On a scale of 1 to 10, how Christ-like is your response to suffering?
How can you become more like him?

Working Together

All of us must quickly carry out the tasks assigned us by the one who sent me, because there is little time left before night falls and all work comes to an end. With those words, Jesus, always the teacher, was proclaiming what a songwriter centuries later would make famous in a hymn that we commonly sing today:

Work while the dew is sparkling, Work mid springing flowers;
Work when the day grows brighter, Work in the glowing sun;
Work, for the night is coming, when man's work is done."
(Annie L. Coghill, "Work for the Night is Coming")

Leon Miller was given a hero's send off today. A man most Americans have never heard of, Leon traveled all over the world as Senior Economist for the World Bank, helping nations mired in poverty and struggling with hunger and disease. He had a monumental task to be sure, yet family and friends remember Leon as a devoted husband and deeply caring father, who literally gave his life serving others. At his memorial service, his pastor, family, and friends honored an incredibly hard worker. Leon drove countless of miles over Christmas holidays, delivering Angel Tree presents to kids whose parents were incarcerated. He visited countless prisoners in jail, telling them about Jesus and praying for them. He visited the hospitalized and homebound, and drove others to doctors' appointments. Leon and his wife Jackie served for many years as altar ministers and marriage counselors. He never waited to be asked but volunteered to help his church family anytime and anywhere. This good man was used by the Lord to bring many of his wayward children to salvation. Now, God has welcomed him home with the words we all hope one day to hear: "Well done, my good and faithful servant."

For reflection:
Think of a time you pitched in to help others,
when you helped God with his work?
How did it make you feel?
Will you seek more opportunities to partner with God?

When God Helps You

As in the case of the blind man who was healed, people today are still amazed when God reaches down and does something defying both logic and science. This happened to a friend, Emily Durham. Emily plays the piano for "hymn sings" at four local nursing homes. Years before, she was diagnosed with thyroid cancer. The diagnosis was confirmed by several biopsies which found papillary carcinoma. Emily immediately called her minister, plus her family and friends, asking them to pray for her.

"We were all storming heaven," she recalls.

Doctors removed her thyroid, expecting to follow-up with three days of isolation in the hospital for radiation treatments. When they rechecked pathology results from the removed thyroid, they could find no cancer. She was completely clear, cancer free!

Her doctor was dumbfounded. "I must have made a mistake in the diagnosis," he apologized.

"No, you didn't, doctor," Emily assured him. "You could not find any cancer because my church and friends were praying for me, I was praying, and God healed me!"

Doctors may fail to understand what happens—or find it hard to acknowledge when God does what they cannot. Their best explanation: "Our diagnosis must have been wrong." But when the cured person is showing them their X-rays and saying, "Look at me now!" how can they deny it?

That's why it's so important to tell others what God has done for you. Never underestimate the power of your testimony to convince someone what God can do for them. Emily will gladly tell you, *Jesus is still passing by*!

For reflection:
Has God healed you or someone you know?
Are you telling others who may need to hear it?

INVALID AT BETHESDA POOL

(Gospel account in John 5:1-47)

Jesus returned to Jerusalem for one of the Jewish holy days. Inside the city, near the Sheep Gate, was the pool of Bethesda with five covered porches. Crowds of sick people, including the lame, blind, and paralyzed, lay on these porches. According to tradition, from time to time an angel of the Lord would come down and stir up the waters. The first sick person into the pool when the angel came would be healed.

One of the men lying there had been an invalid for 38 years. When Jesus saw him and learned how long he'd suffered, he asked him, "Do you want to get well?"

"I can't, sir," the man said, "for I have no one to help me. When the angel comes and I try to get into the water, someone else always beats me."

Jesus told him, "Stand up, pick up your mat, and walk."

Instantly, the man was healed. He picked up his mat and began walking!

Background

When Jesus saw the man who'd been lying sick 38 years, he asked him, "Would you like to get well?" What a strange question! But, think of it from this perspective: The man obviously had family or friends who brought him to the pool every day. Their sympathy was comforting; their devotion assured him he was loved and valued. He had no responsibilities. So, the question was a legitimate one. Maybe you know someone at peace with their infirmity, content to let others provide for them.

Likewise, until alcoholics or drug addicts "bottom out," treatment experts say, it's almost impossible to help them. But when they see and understand their sad future, it's a wake-up call that may persuade them to fight harder. Maybe you've heard the term, "I'm sick and tired of being sick and tired!"

Another challenge for one wanting to get well is: Are you willing to let someone help you? Here Jesus found someone willing to be helped.

Similarly, a person separated from God must also want to be helped. If someone is loving his sin, he's not ready or willing to give it up. When the Holy Spirit touches his heart, however, he's convicted, and the gospel gains a foothold.

Now, when the man rolled up his mat and walked away, you'd think all kinds of praise and hallelujahs would break out. Instead, all hell broke loose.

"Beware of these experts in religion," Jesus warned his followers. Sure enough, they jumped on the man who was healed.

"You can't work on the Sabbath. It's illegal to carry that sleeping mat!"

He replied, "The man who healed me said to me, 'Pick up your sleeping mat and walk.'"

They learned the miracle worker was Jesus. So, they began harassing him. Jesus replied, "My Father never stops working, so why should I?" Blinded by hatred and fear of losing their coveted positions of authority, the religious headhunters tried all the more to kill him.

Have you noticed how violently this ungodly world despises Jesus—that his mere name turns them into crucifiers, decapitators, and murderers? Why?

What was it about Jesus that sent his detractors into a killing frenzy? Was breaking the Sabbath a crime worthy of death? Was his popularity threatening them? It seems his claim to be the Son of God was the final straw. They were incensed. You can imagine them muttering, "He spoke of God as his father—this illegitimate bastard child with no father."

Jesus should have seen it coming. Indeed, he did see it coming, but he was not about to shut up or sit down. He chose to tell them the truth, tell it to their faces. "I assure you, the Son can do nothing by himself. He does only what he sees the Father doing for the Father loves the Son and tells him everything he is doing."

What else could you say, Lord, to infuriate them?

"And the Son will do far greater things than healing this man. You will be astonished—he will even raise from the dead anyone he wants to..."

Now, Jesus had handed them a hanging rope! They had a bogus "crime" to charge him with. In their evil eyes and wicked hearts, he'd committed blasphemy. Making himself equal to God was a sin punishable by death. The inconvenient fact that it was true did not deter the murderers. To those who love darkness, Jesus is an affront to everything they stand for. He gets in their way—and in their face! Like sandpaper against the grain, he rubs them the wrong way.

Jesus had still not finished shaming them with the truth they so deeply hated. Try to imagine their contorted faces, teeth bared, holding their breath, turning purple, when Jesus told them this:

"And the Father leaves all judgment to his Son, so that everyone will honor the Son, just as they honor the Father. But if you refuse to honor the Son, then you are certainly not honoring the Father who sent him. I assure you, those who listen to my message and believe in God who sent me have eternal life. They will never be condemned for their sins but they have already passed from death into life. Indeed, the Father has given his Son authority to judge every person. Even the dead in their graves will hear the voice of God's Son, and they will rise again. Those who listen will live."

Not much wiggle room there!

Life Applications

Do You Want to Get Well?

A brilliant man we once knew was rapidly rising into management at the former U.S. Atomic Energy Commission. His future was bright, but he developed a drinking problem, causing everything to start crumbling. He was counseled to no avail. His family organized an intervention meeting.

We confronted him with the facts: "You've lost your job, you've lost your wife and home, and you've fallen asleep smoking in bed, setting fire to your bed in your rented apartment." He was having none of it. "I'm from Missouri, I don't need help. I can do this on my own." He kept drinking and denying his plight until his liver gave out and he died.

On the other hand, another man we knew abandoned his wife and two little girls, was drinking heavily, and showed no signs of remorse. His father-in-law invited him to church one evening. He came while still intoxicated. God used something in the message to penetrate his heart. When the altar call came, he almost ran to the front, crying and asking for forgiveness. His whole life turned around. He stopped drinking, then smoking, and then he quit cursing. Today he is a leader and lay speaker in his church. He decided he wanted to get well.

For reflection:
Are you at peace with God? If not, do you want to get well?
What lifestyle changes would be required; are you willing to make them?

Where are God's Angels of Mercy Today?

Do you know anyone fighting mental, physical, or psychological infirmities with no one to help? You've heard it said, "God helps those who help themselves." That may be good pop psychology, but it's not biblical. What is true is that God delights in helping those who cannot help themselves.

Jimmy Bennett never imagined himself as an angel of mercy. When he was three years old, his parents separated. He and his siblings were taken from their mother. Two years later, she took her own life by overdosing on drugs. His father was an abusive alcoholic who grew pot in his backyard. Jimmy's childhood was filled with terror and constant fighting. As he describes it, "When I was 12 years old, my brother kicked a can of burning gasoline on me, and I became a human torch. Two-thirds of my body suffered third-degree burns. To save my life, the doctors literally skinned me alive to remove the dead skin."

To numb the pain inside—the shame and embarrassment—Jimmy turned to drugs. He and a friend decided to rob some drug dealers. They ransacked their home, took their money and credit cards, and used their crack cocaine until they were caught and arrested.

"I was facing a total of 350 years in prison. My bail was set at a half-million dollars. I had become a violent criminal, using my burn scars to intimidate other inmates. Locked in solitary confinement for my angry rages and beating other prisoners, I was at the lowest point in my life."

"One day a little old man came to my prison cell and told me God loved me, that he sent his Son Jesus to die for my sins, and that I could have a personal relationship with him. He asked me if he could pray with me. What did I have to lose? So, I said yes. That man's visit changed my life forever. I asked God to forgive me of all my sins and come into my life."

Jimmy and his wife Hulda are now missionaries in Czechia, with five beautiful children. They run kids' camps for orphans and tell spiritually-starved children about Jesus.

Praise be to God, Father of the fatherless! No one who turns to the Lord will be forsaken. If you know and love God, you can never say, "I have no one to help me."

Jimmy shows his burn scars to anyone who can stand to look—then tells them his remarkable story. He will gladly tell you, *Jesus is still passing by.*

For reflection:
How can you become an angel of mercy to one hopeless soul?
Will you tell someone who feels abandoned what the man told Jimmy?

You Can be Someone's Angel

Most Americans likely never heard of Agnes-Marie Valois, but in Canada and France her name is revered. This is her unlikely story.

Sister Valois, who died last month at 103, became known as the "Angel of Dieppe" by caring for nearly 2,000 wounded Canadian soldiers after they were taken as prisoners of war by German forces in World War II. Trained as a nurse, she worked for the French military and in surgical wards before and during the war.

"They once held a gun up to her", a Canadian officer later recalled, "trying to force her to treat their wounded Germans first but she ignored their orders."

When her patients died, Sister Agnes helped arrange for their burial in a local cemetery. One of those wounded warriors even asked her to kiss him as if she were his mother. He died soon after she obliged his request.

Years after the war, Sister Agnes was awarded the French Legion of Honor. She often attended the reunions of "My Canadian soldiers" at Dieppe.

"I remember all my Canadians", she once said. "They're like my family because they were trying to liberate France."

Shrugging off her own well-deserved accolades, she would point back to her soldiers. "They were all very brave."

For reflection:
How has the Lord changed you?
What keeps people today from hearing and responding to the gospel?
How can you become an "angel of mercy" to help them?

A GENTILE WOMAN'S CHILD

(Gospel account in Matthew 15:21-28; Mark 7:24-30)

Jesus went to the vicinity of Tyre, where a Canaanite woman came to him pleading, "Have mercy on me, O Lord, Son of David! For my daughter has a demon in her, and it's severely tormenting her."

Jesus gave her no reply. His disciples urged him to send her away. "Tell her to leave," they said. "She's bothering us with all her begging." Sensitive souls, right?

Then Jesus said to the woman, "I was sent to help the people of Israel, God's lost sheep, not the Gentiles."

But she came and worshipped him, pleading again, "Lord, help me!"

Again, he protested, "It's not right to take the children's bread and toss it to their dogs."

"Yes, Lord," she agreed, "but even puppies eat the crumbs that fall from their master's table."

Her reply seemed to astonish the Lord, blowing away any further thought of refusal.

"Woman, great is your faith," he told her. "Your request is granted." And her daughter was instantly healed.

BACKGROUND

Mom was desperate for her beloved child, who was being severely tormented. She was determined not to be put off by society's rigid "do's and don'ts." She was risking public disgrace, rejection, and humiliation by approaching this Jewish rabbi for help. Yet, her daughter had been stolen from her by this possession, and she would do anything to get her back.

The disciples were likely dumbfounded when Jesus befriended a Gentile (non-Jew)—especially one of Canaanite heritage. The Canaanites had fought the Israelites furiously when the Israelites entered the Promised Land and remained one of their most savage and troublesome enemies.

The good news Jesus was proclaiming traveled fast: "The Kingdom of God is near." And, he was performing miraculous signs and wonders. News of a heaven-sent healer flashed like lightning in a dark sky. The kingdom of heaven was indeed at hand. People were astounded to learn God is for people and not against them—that he's not willing that any should perish but that all will come to have knowledge of God.

Jesus said to the Canaanite, "Woman, I must first help my own people. It's not right to take the children's food and toss it to their dogs."

Why such a harsh-sounding response? Jesus was sent first to God's chosen people the Jews. "He came to his own but his own received him not."

This was true of the majority, yet some Jews were persuaded by the Nazarene. Even two honored members of the high council, Joseph of Arimathea and Nicodemus who came to Jesus at night, became secret followers. They fought past their fears, asking Pilate for his crucified body, then embalmed it with spices, and lovingly laid it in a tomb.

As the story unfolds, this encounter with a Gentile lady, a hated Canaanite, shows us that God has not excluded Gentiles and foreigners. This mother conceded Jesus' point—his first duty was to God's chosen people. Yet, she was not giving up her dreams. Something deep inside was telling her Jesus was a man of uncensored compassion. So, she persisted, "But sir, even the puppies under the table are given scraps from the children's plates." Her stubborn faith was rewarded.

LIFE APPLICATIONS

How Far Would You Go?

The same good news Immanuel brought from heaven is still electrifying, still changing peoples' lives and their eternity. Have you heard it, believed it, and been "born again" by this life-changing truth, that the Lamb of God takes away the sins of the world? It's a text message from God that changes everything, and it's addressed to you.

Today Christians around the world are being targeted for persecution. "The stabbing death of a priest is only the tip of an iceberg," according to a recent report from the American Bible Society. Believers are threatened, beaten, driven from their homes, imprisoned, and even murdered. More than 200 million Christians suffered extreme persecutions in 50 countries last year, the ABS reported. Sadly, missionaries, priests, nurses, and relief workers are often targeted.

These brave soldiers of the cross, facing death every day, are bringing the gospel to some of the most inhospitable places on earth: Muslim nations, communist Europe, India and Pakistan, North Korea, Iraq, Iran, Egypt, Syria, and many others. The Bible says, "Blessed are the feet of them who bring good news." They're depending on our prayers for safety as they carry the gospel into these danger-fraught lands.

Who can deny that *Jesus is still passing by?*

For reflection:
When have you violated traditions or rules to help someone?
How far would you go—will you risk ridicule or danger?

Redeeming Friends and Enemies Alike

That same good news Immanuel brought from heaven is still electrifying, still changing peoples' lives and their eternity. Chuck Colson was known as President Nixon's hatchet man. By his own admission, "I would have stepped on my own grandmother's grave to get ahead." He was charged and convicted of criminal activities, found himself stripped of his White House trappings of power, and sitting in a lonely prison cell. Senator Mark Hatfield and other Christians on Capitol Hill decided to share their faith with Colson. He was receptive. He repented and received Christ as his Savior. The former hatchet man today has a worldwide prison ministry that is finding and redeeming thousands of lost souls.

For reflection
What type of person do you find it difficult to befriend?
Will this miracle encourage you to push past society's stereotypes?

Stubborn Faith Rewarded

One day Daniel, a young newly married Jewish man was milking cows in an Israeli agricultural commune when he slipped, seriously injuring his back. When it didn't heal, his doctors ordered surgery but accidently severed some vital nerves, leaving him paralyzed. One day as he was idly flipping through his television channels at home, he turned to the 700 Club, a

Christian ministry program, and heard of people being healed by accepting Jesus into their lives and having fellow believers pray for them.

Daniel was skeptical but kept watching the program. When the host invited viewers to pray to receive Christ into their lives, Daniel overcame his fears and responded. Listening to a prophetic speaker one day, Daniel sensed he was about to be healed. Sure enough, feeling soon began returning to his paralyzed legs. When he was examined by his Jewish doctors they proclaimed it to be a medical miracle. "This is not a medical miracle. This is Yeshua!" Daniel told them. That was too much for his Jewish doctors.

He began calling himself a Messianic Jew, telling people that Jesus had healed him. The agricultural commune leaders threw Daniel and his wife out of the commune, giving them ten days to leave. "Had God not made a way, we would've been out in the streets penniless," he says.

That was not to be. Someone soon handed him an envelope. When he opened it, he couldn't believe his eyes. It contained two airline tickets and a scholarship to attend Bible school in Dallas, Texas. His dream is to return to Israel one day to proclaim the Messiah who saves and heals.

For Reflection:
Who has the most long-suffering faith of anyone you've known?
When have you personally seen stubborn faith rewarded?

HEALING BLIND BARTIMAEUS

(Gospel account in Matthew 20:29-34; Mark 10:46-52; Luke 18:35-43 (note: Matthew records two blind men in this encounter)

Jesus and his disciples came next to Jericho. As they were leaving that dusty town, a blind man Bartimaeus sat by the roadside begging. This miracle recounts how Jesus restored his sight.

When Bartimaeus heard the noisy crowd going by, he asked, "What's happening?"

Someone told him, "Jesus of Nazareth is passing by."

Bartimaeus then cried out, "Jesus, Son of David, have mercy on me!"

Those who fancied themselves Jesus' palace guards rebuked the beggar. "Be quiet!" they scolded him.

But he shouted even louder, "Son of David, have mercy on me!"

When he heard Bartimaeus, Jesus stopped and ordered the man brought to him. Jesus asked him, "What do you want me to do for you?"

He replied, "Teacher, I want to see again."

Jesus told him, "Go, your faith has made you well."

At once he was able to see and followed Jesus down the road.

Background

Would you consider a blind man begging handouts to be poor? So would I. But, first inclinations are often wrong. Bartimaeus was about to receive the most precious gift a blind man could dream of—his sight restored—without paying even a widow's mite.

Was he poor in God's sight? Apparently not. So, to be rich in God's sight or people's opinion, which would you choose? The Biggest Loser is the person--no matter how rich--who lives and dies without God.

Our Lord spoke an uncomfortable truth when he reminded us we can't serve both God and mammon. He seemed to be saying: "Take your pick."

The crowd saw a worthless derelict, an object of scorn. Jesus saw a fellow human of great worth. Why so? The Bible gives us a hint: Man looks on the outside to judge a person, but God looks on the inside.

How quickly the clamoring crowd changes! As soon as Jesus stops and calls to Bartimaeus, those who were screaming at him to shut up and go away now become his cheerleaders. "Cheer up! On your feet! He's calling you."

Beware the fickle whims of people! One day you're lower than a snake's belly, the next day you're riding high in the saddle. Just remember, the same ones who helped you mount that white stallion may be the same ones dragging you off, mixing a bucket of hot tar and feathers in your honor!

Thanks be to God who doesn't change like shifting shadows. He's not here today and gone tomorrow—not your friend on Sunday but conniving and treacherous on Monday. His steady hand is always in arms reach—when you need it, where you need it—and no matter how often. If you're his, then he is yours. The gospel of Mark doesn't leave us in suspense as to what happened to this blind beggar. Here's the rest of the story: As soon as Bartimaeus received his new pair of eyes, he followed Jesus down the road, praising God.

Imagine the impact this man's story had on family and community. And what do you suppose Bartimaeus would say to us if he could bridge the centuries? That the Spirit of the Nazarene is alive and well—still meeting humanity's deepest needs? Would he tell you those crying out to Jesus will be helped? That faith in Jesus makes one whole? That he gives us garments of praise to cure our spirits of heaviness?

Would he testify that *Jesus is still passing by*? That he knows your name, where you live, and what you need? Indeed. And Bartimaeus would likely plead with us, "Don't let cynics steal your miracle!"

When Jesus asked him, "What can I do for you?" Bartimaeus was ready.

"Lord, I want to see," he replied. Jesus said to him, "All right, you can see! Your faith has healed you." Instantly he received his sight and followed Jesus, praising God.

What did the fickle crowd learn that day—and did it affect their lives? Luke's account gives us hope because he includes this final word: "When all the people saw it, they also praised God."

They learned every person has worth and dignity in God's eyes. The very fact that God created you, loves you, wants to spend eternity with you—gives you value beyond words.

You can stop searching for meaning and worth. It's God's free gift to you.

Life Applications

Heaven's Perspective

Do you know people with the sympathies of a chameleon? Do your own loyalties sometimes shift with the political winds?

Rosa, a lady who cleaned the floors at our church fell ill and died suddenly. We attended her memorial service expecting the crowd to be sparse. The sanctuary was overflowing. The pastor told of how she would often put down her broom or mop and come into his study, asking for prayer.

"After I prayed for her, she would begin praying for me. Such spirit-filled prayers, full of God's promises. I got the feeling she often asked me to pray for her just so she could pray for me."

When the pastor allowed time for people to share what Rosa had meant to them, the stories went on and on.

"What a beautiful tribute to a humble servant!" my wife remarked after the service. "You would have thought she was royalty."

You may have heard the saying, "She doesn't sell for what she's worth!" Maybe you're not young, rich, and beautiful. Or maybe you're one of the few "lucky" ones. But, is that a decent way of determining one's worth? Aren't you glad heaven's perspective is different—that God doesn't judge you as people do?

For reflection:
By what measure do you judge others?
How can we begin seeing others as Jesus does?

A Servant's Heart

George Jernigan told the lucky lady he proposed to, "If you marry me, I promise you that I will spend the rest of my life trying to make you happy." In the decades that followed, Mary Alice saw that promise gloriously fulfilled. Her body was ravished by diabetes, she lost most of her eyesight, suffered amputation of one of her legs, was in a long protracted comma until doctors feared she had suffered brain damage. Through it all, George never left her side. He became an expert in administering her many medications and injections. He helped her dress and eat and learn to walk again with her artificial leg. He bathed her and helped with her hygiene. He took her every week to her hair appointments, cooked her meals, and served them. He did her laundry, housekeeping, and grocery shopping; took her to buy new clothes. He loved, cherished, provided and defended her—just as he'd promised on his knees. Mary Alice told everyone , "George is my miracle". When God finally called her home, George seemed to have lost all reason to go on--until the Lord gave him another wonderful companion to love, cherish, and live to make happy. George truly has a servant's heart. Some of us struggle with that.

Dot needs me at the most inconvenient times! Does she not realize that you readers are waiting to hang onto my every word?

"Bennett, did you take out the trash? When was the last time you cleaned the commodes?" Bless her heart, she has no clue what gems of wisdom you'll be missing!

Remember Jesus warned us, "I, your Messiah, came not to be served but to serve. And you likewise who want to be first must be a slave of all!"

Sounds like some of us need to ask for more of a servant's heart.

"Okay, Dot, I'm coming!"

For reflection:
Examine your past week. Have your actions shown a servant's heart? How might you become more like Jesus?

What Gives Us True Worth

John and Susan were happy parents of three adorable boys. Most days, after completing his duty as a Montgomery County police captain, John could be seen outside tossing a football, or shooting basketball hoops or just rough-housing with T.J., Michael, and Matthew. Great neighbors, friendly and outgoing, volunteering to shovel sidewalks, mow lawns, and assist those needing a helping hand, this family was living the American dream.

So, they were excited when Susan became pregnant again. Maybe God was going to give the boys a little sister to love and cherish. When Susan went for a sonogram, her doctor came back looking troubled. "Your fetus is a boy, but he will be born with Down's syndrome. You and your husband need to think about what this will involve and decide what to do. It's your choice."

True to their Catholic faith, the Fitzgeralds began praying for wisdom and guidance. John explained at the time, "We know we're facing a life-changing decision. If we bring this child into the world, we realize things will never be the same for us. We'd never be able to get away on our own for vacations. We'd never be able to retire as most parents do. As long as we'd live, we'd be responsible for this child. But, if we choose to terminate the pregnancy for our own convenience, how could we ever look ourselves in the mirror?" They chose life for Danny.

When Danny finally arrived, the whole family fell in love with him immediately. His brothers could hardly let him out of their sight. They showered him with so much love it was heartwarming to see. Soon, Danny began responding with sheer joy.

Today it would be impossible to describe what he means to this family. His brothers eventually went away to college, but they still return for Danny's birthdays and for every other possible opportunity. Danny has become the neighborhood pied piper, giving out super hugs and greetings.

When Matthew brought his first girlfriend home to meet the family, Danny fell head over heels in love with her. Danny stuck to them like glue. When Matthew moved on to college, leaving her behind, Danny was inconsolable.

Danny loves the outdoors, greeting everyone with his arms lifted high, rejoicing at life. He speaks his own language, one overflowing with love. Danny is not easily offended, holds no grudges, and never thinks ill of anyone. Loyal, kind, and trusting, he is his mom's poster child for 1 COR 13:13, "There are three things that will last forever: faith, hope, and love—and the greatest of these is love."

Susan and John followed their heart and did the right thing. God has filled their home with so much joy you can feel it when you walk in the door. "Danny has taught us what true value and worth are all about."

For reflection:
How would you characterize your true value and worth?
What did you learn from Danny's story?

A WIDOW'S DEAD SON

(Gospel account in Luke 7:11-17)

Jesus went to a town called Nain with his disciples and a large crowd following. As they approached the town gate, pallbearers were carrying out a dead man in a casket. He was the only son of his widowed mother. A big funeral procession was following the casket—relatives and friends mourning for the son and his grieving mom.

When Jesus saw her, his heart went out to her, and he said, "Don't cry." Then, he went up and touched the coffin, and those carrying it stood still.

"Young man, I say to you, get up!" he commanded. The dead man sat up and began to talk, and Jesus gave him back to his mother.

Background

Did this look like a small problem? Did the grieving mother see it as a mere bump in the road? What was the crowd of mourners thinking as they trailed her out of town? How would she survive—this lonely widow—with no safety net to catch her? No food stamps, no welfare checks, no Medicare or social security in those days.

Then, Jesus came passing by! Suddenly, her worse nightmare became God's opportunity. The widow's mountain was too high to climb until the one who made the mountains showed up. No hope until Jesus—no problem for Jesus!

We need to internalize this: God delights in conquering our impossibilities. When we're weak, he's strong, when we're powerless, he's dynamite powerful. God glories in helping his people, and we learn to trust him more. The Lord told Paul, "My grace is all you need, for my power is strongest when you are weak." (2 COR. 12:9a, TEV)

In our darkest hours, we wonder, "Who's going to be there for me?" When the bottom falls out, when your family is too busy with their own problems, when your friends move away, and neighbors don't even know your name, what then?

This poor widow had no more sons. She was left destitute—all alone in a world too busy to notice. Oh, they cared—they would grieve with her at the graveside. They might even bring her a few meals. Yet, soon life would engulf them and they would be too busy surviving to remember her.

But, here's the good news: The Lord notices and cares. What do you suppose the coffin-bearers were thinking when Jesus walked over and put his hand on the casket? Imagine the people's amazement when this stone-dead corpse suddenly started breathing, opened his eyes, sat up and asked, "What's going on?"

A fresh-dug grave gave up its victory. Jesus proved once again the Son of Man has been given power over death. The Father verified the Son of Man is also the Son of God. The Lord demonstrated his love for hurting people. God notices, God cares, God acts—no wonder they call it amazing grace!

This dream-like encounter with the Nazarene left no doubt in the widow's mind who Jesus was. Neither was her son left wondering. The crowd was blown away, his disciples convinced.

A heartwarming story most will agree, but how does it apply to you? Well, sooner or later we may be standing in the widow's shoes—alone, forgotten, bereft of family and friends, with no one to help us but Jesus. You need to know, "Can I count on him?"

People hearing the story secondhand were of differing persuasions—some became believers and followed Jesus; others were almost persuaded; still others remained unconvinced.

Satan's hand-picked religious bigots were of one accord: He's stealing our thunder. We must do everything in our power to discredit him in the eyes of the people.

Would you agree that public opinions of Jesus today are not much different? Some are still wandering around in a valley of decision. Some are willing to die rather than deny him. Others think they're doing God a favor to decapitate the "infidels."

Life Applications

Your Impossibility is God's Opportunity

Lady Liberty welcomed Justin Demalo, an immigrant from the Democratic Republic of Congo, and he entered what appeared to be a good career with a prestigious Wall Street banking firm in New York City. His new world began to crumble, however, when his wife left him. Soon after, he witnessed the tragic destruction of the Twin Towers on 9/11. Justin's nearby office was temporarily closed and his department transferred the business to Bournemouth, England. After unsuccessful efforts to reassign Justin and his colleagues to other locations, the company offered them severance packages. They found themselves standing in unemployment lines. Justin's life spiraled from American Dream to American nightmare. Shortly after 9/11, Justin had become a born again Christian, but it was time to leave the Big Apple. Alone, jobless, and soon to be homeless, he turned his distraught soul to heaven in a universal cry, "Help me, Lord!" and the Lord answered.

Justin turned to relatives living in the Washington, D.C. metropolitan area, and they opened their door, taking him in. Meanwhile, the economy spiraled downward, with the financial sector especially hard hit. Yet, Justin persisted, knocking on doors until a lower level position opened. He enrolled in night graduate school to make himself more marketable.

Slowly, things turned for the better, but Justin was still alone and lonely. On a trip back to the Congo, he met a lovely Christian lady who spoke French, the official language of the country. They fell in love and decided to marry, and he brought her back with him to the United States.

In Maryland, Justin soon joined a local church and found a men's fellowship group, which made him feel loved and welcomed. Today, he and his wife Yvette are reaching to help others, and both are blessed with employment. He delights in giving God the glory, telling anyone who will listen that your impossibility is Christ's opportunity.

For reflection:
Has God shown up to aid you when you were in dire need?
Will you acknowledge your weaknesses, asking for his grace?

God Resurrects and Restores

Louis and Renee had been battling addictions for most of their lives when God began calling them to freedom. They met at a halfway house after completing intense treatments for addiction to alcohol, cocaine, and other illegal drugs. They fell in love and began living together, but God had other plans for them. He called them into a Spirit-filled church where they committed their lives to Christ. Hearing strong bible-based messages convicted them of their sinful lifestyle so they decided to live separately until they were married. They worked at getting to know each other better and Christ more intimately. When they finally married the way God ordained, blessings began to flow. Renee had been told due to her past lifestyle of additions, prostitution, and abusing her body, she would never be able to conceive, let alone give birth to a healthy child. Because they honored God, though, he did the impossible for them. Renee conceived on their honeymoon. Daughter Grace is their daily reminder of God's tender mercy. Louis is the true spiritual leader of this miracle family. Renee now ministers to other women, homeschools their daughter, and lovingly encourages and respects her husband. They love serving together at their church and 13-year-old Grace helps little children in the nursery and is beginning to lead worship music.

"If you would've asked us what we were praying for in our darkest days, we would've said, 'I just want to make it through this day not having to use drugs!' God did exceedingly more than we could have imagined. Only God saves, heals, delivers, and redeems. Only God can take lives so broken and shattered and not only make them whole but also make them productive. He turned our mess into a message of Christ's resurrection grace."

For reflection:
What "dead dreams" has God resurrected for you
(e.g., broken friendships, lost opportunities restored)?

Who is This Man?

Mr. Robey was an elderly gentleman who lived alone with his bedridden wife when friend John and I began visiting him weekly as part of a Friendly Visitors program. He responded immediately, and soon we were helping him plant and till his summer tomato gardens. Over coffee, we listened to his shaggy-dog stories, but one topic was off-limits. Mr. Robey was very angry with God, blaming Him for his wife's stroke and paralysis. For 17 years he had been her sole caregiver, lovingly feeding her only pureed food, and changing her diapers. He was terribly bitter that a good and godly lady would have to suffer so. He would allow us to pray for her only after he left the room.

Time went by until one day Mr. Robey backed into a lady's car while out buying groceries. Instead of throwing a fit, this gracious Christian lady was only concerned that he may have been injured. She insisted on following him home, came in and met his wife, and began visiting and praying for her. Slowly, Mr. Robey's wall of bitterness began to crumble as their new friend witnessed to him of how much God loved them and wanted to take them both to heaven. Mr. Robey was brought to his senses by the Christlike compassion and mercy of one dear saint who took the time to befriend them and show him the love of our Risen Lord. Both Mr. and Mrs. Robey are today in paradise with Jesus, enjoying perfect health in their heavenly mansion.

For reflection:
Have you sorted this through—the identity of Christ?
What do you need God to restore for you (e.g., faith, career, health, a broken friendship, a severed relationship)?

LAZARUS RAISED FROM DEATH

(Gospel account in John 11:1-44)

A man named Lazarus was gravely ill. He was the brother of Mary and Martha, all good friends of Jesus. The Lord was often a guest in their home, dining with them and spending the night on his frequent trips to the Holy City.

His sisters sent word, "Lord, the one you love is sick."

They expected him to rush to their brother's side, but Jesus stayed where he was, ministering for two more days. Lazarus died and was buried. Finally, Jesus said to his disciples, "Our friend Lazarus has fallen asleep, but now I will go and wake him up."

Thinking Jesus meant Lazarus was enjoying a good night's rest, the disciples responded, "Lord, if he's sleeping that means he's getting better."

Then Jesus told them plainly, "Lazarus is dead. And for your sake, I'm glad I wasn't there, because this will give you another opportunity to believe in me. Come, let's go to him."

When Jesus finally arrived, his friend had been in the tomb four days.

Jesus called to him in a loud voice, "Lazarus, come forth!" The dead man came out—his hands and feet bound up in the grave cloth, his face muffled in a head swath.

Jesus said to Mary and Martha, "Take off his grave clothes, and let him go."

Background

Some things are beyond human help. This was certainly true of Lazarus. He was dying. He knew it; Mary and Martha knew it. No doctor had been able to cure him; in fact, he was fading fast. Mary and Martha did the only thing left to do. They appealed to God and sent for Jesus. Surely, they reasoned, the Master would not refuse their desperate call. He would drop everything and rush to his good friend's side.

Yet, Jesus tarried. He failed to show up as soon as they expected. Still, Mary and Martha's faith saved their brother's life. They learned that God doesn't always answer our prayers the way we're expecting.

They assumed that Jesus would drop everything and come to rescue his beloved friend. Isn't that what you would expect?

Jesus could have rushed to Lazarus—or simply spoken a word long-distance as he did for the Centurion's servant. He did neither but continued his ministry, despite his friend's approaching death.

Mary and Martha were frantic. Did Jesus get their message? What could be so important he would let Lazarus die by tarrying? Did he no longer love them? Had they done something to offend him? Were they paying for some unknown sin? On and on, their fevered minds raced—trying to sort out what they saw as a rebuff—certainly a nonchalant attitude. Yet Jesus waited two more days. Why?

"This is going to happen for the glory of God!" he told his disciples. Do you suppose they understood? Not likely. But as we see later, Jesus had something more wonderful than they could imagine in store.

What's the takeaway for us? When you lift your needs to God—simply trust him. Leave the details to him. He alone decides when and how to answer—and his ways and timing always prove to be perfect.

Life Applications

Our Friend or Last Resort?

Dot spent 25 years bringing music to nursing home residents. She loved her job and felt God was using her to bless some of society's most forgotten and lonely ones. After many years, a young supervisor came in who decided she needed to change everything although the nurses and staff loved Dot's programs and their activity department consistently earned the highest evaluations from the state health inspectors. Her dream job became a nightmare. She could do nothing to please her new boss. She tried everything to adjust and win her confidence. Nothing worked. She began crying out to God to soften the lady's heart and help her to see how much the residents loved the music. This churning turmoil went on until Dot didn't think she could take it any longer. She was seriously thinking of giving up when one morning the lady bounced in with a big smile and announced, "Guess what, Dottie! I've found a new job with a promotion and higher pay and will be leaving in two weeks! Isn't that great?"

Dot assured her, "Yes, that's wonderful, and I'm so happy for you." She really meant it. Silently, she was also thanking God for solving her "impossible" problem!

For reflection:
How would you characterize your intimacy with Jesus? Do you think of him as your friend, constant companion, or last resort?
Under what circumstances do you appeal to God? To find lost keys, a parking place, promotion, peace, to save loved ones?

God's Timing or Ours?

Every miracle Jesus did gave his disciples yet another reason to conclude he was Messiah. Would raising a corpse back to life who'd lain in a tomb four days be convincing to you? And so it is with us. Every miracle Jesus did in the Bible—or that we encounter today—gives us yet another opportunity to trust him. Sometimes it may simply be helping you find something important you've lost. Joy Dawson tells this story in her book, *Forever Ruined for the Ordinary.*

"I had given my mother a pretty blue pen and a tapestry case. When she died, I acquired that pretty blue pen. It became my favorite pen because it was so smooth-flowing; it was the perfect size and color; and besides, it had belonged to someone very precious to me. So, it had sentimental value.

One day at my office I noticed it was missing. I looked everywhere I knew and asked God to help me find it. My husband and secretary joined in the search but it never showed up. Finally, I said to God, 'In your omniscience, you know exactly where it is, and because of your understanding love, I believe you see it is important to me to find it, so, please tell me exactly where it is.' I stopped and listened. Immediately an impression came into my mind, 'It's in the office bathroom.'

I had looked carefully in the bathroom earlier and had seen nothing. It seemed the most unlikely place, but I have learned to obey that voice. I looked again. I then saw it on the floor in an obscure place, behind the toilet! Only God knows how it got there, and only He could help me find it. At times like this I worship Him for His humility to be involved in my little world."

Has God done that for you—shown unmistakably he wants to help you? To be involved in your joys, sorrows, and challenges? When we get serious with God, he gets serious with us, time after time giving us yet another opportunity to believe.

For reflection:
What has God done for you lately that caused your faith to grow?

His Plan is Greater

A man was nominated for a Presidential appointment to direct a nationwide search for a high-level nuclear waste disposal site. His name was prominently announced in the Washington Post. He thought it would be his dream come true. He began to pray about it. He did not get the job. It turned out to be a confrontational and highly political position, an impossible cauldron. The man selected soon found himself despised by every community, State, and Indian Tribe being considered for the nation's "nuclear dumping grounds".

The man who dreamed of the opportunity saw three distinguished directors fired and fail. What he had dreamed of and prayed for turned out to be a nightmare. God heard his prayers but was not persuaded. By denying his ambition, the Lord saved him and his family untold sorrows.

For reflection:
Have you thought you knew best about something, prayed about it, but God gave you a different answer that turned out to be so much better?

A WOMAN CRIPPLED 18 YEARS

(Gospel account in Luke 13:10-17)

One Sabbath as Jesus was teaching in the synagogue, a woman showed up who'd been crippled 18 years. Her back was bent double by an evil spirit so she wasn't able to straighten up.

When Jesus saw her, he called her over and said, "Woman, you're healed of your sickness." Then, he touched her and instantly she could stand up perfectly straight.

Background

On this Sabbath we find Jesus worshipping in a synagogue. It was not difficult to track Jesus down on any Sabbath. This was his custom—to find a local house of worship and join them for Scripture reading, praying, and teaching one another about God. Jesus was modeling his Father's commandment, "Remember the Sabbath day to keep it holy." What a wonderful tradition, would you agree? Healthy for body, mind and spirit.

Jesus teaching was interrupted when he noticed a lady so deformed and crippled she couldn't stand or walk upright. Yet, she came to synagogue. What a wonderful legacy this dear lady left us!

Then came a religious leader to criticize and find fault. "There are six days of the week for working," he scolded the crowd. "Come on those days to be healed, not on the Sabbath."

But the Lord cut him off, "You hypocrite! You work on the Sabbath day!" Don't you untie your ox or donkey from their stalls on the Sabbath and lead them out to water? Wasn't it necessary for me, even on the Sabbath day, to free this dear woman from the bondage in which Satan has held her for eighteen years?"

This shamed his enemies. And the people rejoiced in the wonderful thing he did.

Life Applications

Unusual Encounters With Jesus

When this precious handicapped lady was struggling to get to her synagogue that particular Sabbath, she had no idea what God had in store for her. Our daughter Jan bought tickets and arranged for a family tour of the new Museum of the Bible in Washington, D.C.. Since nearby parking is hard to find, we opted to take the subway (Metro).

This presented an unexpected problem because we needed to transport Dot in a portable wheelchair. Because the wheels of a portable wheelchair are small, they kept getting caught between the train and the platform as we were changing trains, before entering and exiting the stations. We were amazed at peoples' responses. Each time this happened, our fellow passengers came to our rescue, helping us lift Dot in the chair and over the gap. Because of these good Samaritans, we all enjoyed the tour and learned that, despite horror stories one hears of rush hour chaos, chivalry is still alive in the big city.

How refreshing to discover miracles in a subway, one's faith in strangers restored, and Jesus riding the Metro!

For reflection:
When have you encountered Jesus in a delightfully surprising way?
Do you agree that he wants to use us as his heart, hands, and feet to others?

Responding to Human Needs

Franklin Graham was a mischievous kid, headstrong and rebellious. In other words, pretty normal for an adolescent energy-driven teenager. The problem for Franklin was, because Billy Graham was his father, people expected the mantle of greatness to fall on him. To say the least, young Franklin was not ready for greatness. What he was ready for was fun and trouble. His dad was gone months at a time around the world on great crusades. His saintly mom had to deal with Franklin's stubborn and determined ways. Franklin got into fights, fell in love with guns, dogs, and rock-n-roll music. Attracted to women, beer, and fast cars, Franklin seemed an unlikely candidate to step into his famous father's shoes. He promised himself one thing he would never do: preach in a crusade. But with his grandfather praying, Billy and Ruth praying, and God knocking on his door, the young rebel didn't stand a chance. Today he stands before presidents and potentates as an ambassador for Christ. However, what really exploded in his heart, once he surrendered his life to God, was the plight of the world's poor, helpless, and homeless. Franklin has poured his mind, body, and soul into serving these hurting ones. Today one will find Samaritans Purse, the international charity he leads, bringing food and life-sustaining supplies, along with hope to the helpless, around the world.

For reflection:
Are you deeply touched—even wounded—by the suffering of others?
Are they so important you can be depended on to come to their aid?

Rejoicing with Others

Lois Harris has invested her life in affirming others. Birthdays, anniversaries, bridal and baby showers, Lois finds a way to honor family and friends, making them feel loved and special. Husband John is her enabler, dropping everything to help Lois do her hospitality thing. For 60 years and counting, they have been the face of Jesus to countless souls. Like the famous lady in *Proverbs*, Lois is a woman of strength and dignity. When she speaks her words are wise and her words are clothed in kindness. She serves her Lord by celebrating his people. She has found favor with God and will be surely praised.

For reflection:
Who cares deeply about you—and vice versa?
Are you quick to rejoice with others, joining in their celebrations?

INSANE MAN IN A GRAVEYARD

(Gospel account in Matthew 8:28-34; Mark 5:1-20; Luke 8:26-39)

The Lord and his disciples rowed across Lake Galilee to the territory of Gerasa. As Jesus stepped from the boat, a man driven insane by an evil spirit ran out from a cemetery to meet him. This man lived among the tombs and had become so violent he couldn't be restrained, even with chains. When he was bound in shackles—as he often was—he snapped the chains from his wrists and smashed the irons. No one was strong enough to overpower or control him. All day and through the night he wandered among the tombs and in the wild hills, screaming and cutting himself with sharp stones. When he saw Jesus from a distance, the wild man ran and fell on his knees in front of him.

"What do you want with me, Jesus, Son of the Most High God? Swear to God that you won't torture me!"

He responded in this way because Jesus had said to him, "Come out of this man, you evil spirit!"

The evil spirit gave a terrible scream, "What are you going to do to me? For God's sake don't torture me!"

Then Jesus asked him, "What is your name?"

"My name is Legion," he replied, "for we are many."

Thereupon, the Lord restored the possessed man's mind and set him free.

Background

Why do you think this super-strong and fearsome man ran to Jesus and fell at his feet? It's a pretty safe bet the demons inside him didn't choose to do so. Yet his afflicted soul needed relief. So, if it were not by Legion's choice, it would seem the power of God compelled Legion to come and surrender. Call it a command performance.

He begged Jesus again and again not to banish him out of the area. Then, pointing out a huge herd of hogs rooting on the hill above the lake, the demons begged, "Send us into those hogs."

Jesus gave them his permission. So, the evil spirits came out of the man and entered the hogs, and then the entire herd of 2,000 plunged down the steep hillside into the lake. The pig herders ran off and reported the exorcism in the town and countryside—including what happened to the pigs. Then the whole town went out to meet Jesus. When they came to Jesus, they saw the man who'd been possessed by demons, sitting there, dressed, and in his right mind.

Those who witnessed the miracle told the villagers arriving later how Jesus exorcised the demons and cured the insane man. The crowd was so overcome with fear they asked Jesus to leave. So, he got back into the boat and left.

The hogs' owners were upset at losing their valuable herd, and the pig herders were out of their job. But the rest of the crowd was sympathetic. The demons inside this man recognized Jesus—confessed that he was the Son of the Most High God. Indeed, the power of Satan and his demons is frightful but limited, subject to God's higher authority. While it's true some people get carried away—seeing a demon under every rock—it's equally true that Satan has been given a limited time to tempt, torment, and afflict God's people.

The man who'd been driven insane by demons and restored by Jesus begged to join the Lord on his crusade. But Jesus said no. "Go back home to your family and tell them what wonderful things God has done for you and how merciful he has been." And the man did.

God is not playing hide-and-seek. His Holy Spirit indwells us to show us the way. Our challenge is often to let go of our cherished plans—and seek only his will. It's really very simple when we stop to think about it: God's plans for us are greater than anything we could hope for or dream up. Why wouldn't we go with God's plan?

Life Applications

Are You Safe?

Jesus obviously spent valuable time and energy responding to a wild man in a graveyard. He was willing to sacrifice 2,000 pigs to free one tortured human being. Let's rejoice that hurting people are priceless to God! Insanity is a frightening disease, and demon possession even more so. A person under demonic attack may lose control of mind, body, and spirit. Murderers sometimes claim, "Voices were telling me to do it." We had such a case in my father's family.

Dad's cousin had an invalid wife who fell down the stairs in their basement one day. "So, I took an ax and killed her," he explained.

My father, a minister, visited Cousin Arthur while he was in jail, awaiting trial for murder. He told my father, "When she fell, I heard a voice from God saying, 'Arthur! You must put her out of her misery!'"

Pleading for sympathy, he asked Daddy, "Ira, you believe me, don't you?" My father told him, "Yes Arthur, I believe you heard a voice. But, it wasn't from God."

Some psychologists and psychiatrists deny that evil spirits exist—or that they have power to "possess" human beings. Their medical and scientific training does not equip them to deal with what the Bible calls mighty evil powers in high places.

Don't count Dr. Richard Gallagher among the doubters. A scientist educated at Princeton, he was trained in psychiatry at Yale and in psychoanalysis at Columbia. For 25 years, Dr. Gallagher has worked with clergy of many faiths to filter out regular mental illness cases from darker spiritual attacks. A victim under demonic possession, he found, may burst out with astonishing venom and contempt for God, speak in foreign languages, and exhibit enormous strength. (Washington Post, 7/3/16, B.1)

Policemen trying to bring someone on mind-altering drugs under control find it often takes several officers to overpower him. What do you suppose is the source of this supernatural strength?

Here's the good news. Christians need not be victimized by demonic powers because we have access to God's unlimited power. God protects his own.

For reflection:
Have you experienced anyone under spiritual attack?
Have you ever felt spiritually threatened or in danger? (If so, did you sense God's protection?)

Seek Godly Counsel

A troubled young man came to his pastor for counseling. He was blaming his parents for causing his dysfunctional life, his boss for treating him unfairly, and his church family for not understanding his mood swings. He was growing increasingly paranoid and suffering panic attacks. The pastor, who had extensive counseling training, soon recognized his young charge was refusing to take responsibility for anything but insisted on finding someone else to blame for all his problems.

The pastor lovingly asked the young man to bow his head and imagine that he was sitting beside Almighty God on His judgment throne. They both were clothed in black judges' robes, wore identical crowns, and held in their hand judges' gavels.

"Now, I want you to see yourself standing up and coming down off the judgment seat. Now, take off your crown and robe and hand them back to God along with your gavel. Now ask the Lord to forgive you for trying to take over his role. Promise God that beginning today you will leave all judging to Him."

The shock therapy worked because the counseling was both wise and godly.

For reflection:
Do you know anyone needing psychological help?
Will you be proactive in getting them connected
with a professional counselor?

You Also Have Authority

How does this strange tale intersect with you and me? Instead of cowering to demonic powers, let's remember we have the Holy Spirit indwelling us. So, if evil spirits target you, be bold and courageous. Stand on your faith—confront and rebuke them in Jesus' name. God's authority is supreme, unrivaled, and undisputable. Use your God-given authority. Call on the name of Jesus. You're bought by his blood, safe in his arms. Satan has no dominion over you. Don't allow him in your playground.

Shirley visited a new church and decided to join a women's Bible study. The first day the teacher held up a Bible and told the participants, "First of all, you need to understand this is an obsolete book written a long time ago by ignorant old men." When the class was over, Shirley walked out and never went back.

It didn't take her long to see that this teacher was denying *the authority of Holy Scripture.* Was Shirley acting rationally—by voting with her feet?

Some think the idea of demonic attacks is nothing more than ignorant superstition—that science has proven the Scriptures to be outmoded. Malachi Martin, an exorcist highly respected by church authorities, stated in his book, *Hostage to the Devil,* that Satan's greatest victory in the 20th century was to convince most people that he does not exist.

"If you think the Bible is just a mysterious, outdated book, think again," says Phillip Yancey, author and an editor for *Christianity Today.* In fact, it deals in astonishing depth with the issues that trouble us most, he concludes.

For reflection:
Where do you personally turn for counsel (e.g., prayer, scripture, meditation, clergy, friend)?
How would you reach out to someone under spiritual duress?

A SCREAMING DEMON IN THE SYNAGOGUE

(Gospel account in Mark 1:21-28; Luke 4:31-37)

On a Sabbath, Jesus went into the synagogue at Capernaum and began to teach. His message amazed the people because he taught with such great authority.

Just then a man possessed by an evil spirit cried out, "What do you want with us, Jesus of Nazareth? Have you come to destroy us? I know who you are, the Holy One of God!"

"Be quiet!" Jesus thundered. "Come out of him!"

As the awe-struck crowd watched, the evil spirit screamed and threw the man to the floor, shook him violently, but came out without hurting him. In other words, he obeyed the command of a higher power.

Shock gripped the audience, and they began discussing what they'd just seen. "What kind of teaching is this?" they whispered. "It has such authority! Even evil spirits obey his orders!"

Background

News of what Jesus did that day traveled like a wind-whipped wildfire into the towns and countryside of Galilee. On farms and through hills and valleys, the fame of the Nazarene grew. People far and wide wanted to see and hear this great teacher—and to witness his power.

This miracle, as with all Jesus' signs and wonders, was meant to help and heal people—and to validate his message. Such power demands a personal response from all who see it or hear of it. Blessed were those who saw the demon exorcised. More blessed still are those who were not present yet believe God's Word. Decision time had come in Capernaum.

Indeed, the glory, the kingdom, and the power had arrived on earth: Emanuel had come!

You can imagine their excitement: Who is this guy? Where did he learn all this? Slowly, they were putting two and two together. Could it be? Was it possible? Have we lived to see the ancient prophesies fulfilled? Is he the one we've been waiting for to redeem Israel? To most, only one conclusion was possible. His messages and miracles were defeating their doubts.

Demons are indeed fearsome and powerful—until they confront God. Christian, don't negotiate with them. The Holy Spirit lives in you. Jesus will help you fight your spiritual battles. Yes, we face situations when compromise is wise and helpful, but not with evil. Someone has said we can be so open-minded our brain falls out! But, God doesn't negotiate with demons and evil-doers, he shows them the door.

Jesus said of himself: "I came to do my Father's will." So, what did that look like? Just what we see here—Emanuel helping people. This day finds him telling the good news and inviting God's wandering sheep to reconnect with him. The miraculous exorcism was a show-stopper but not the main event.

What did the people see in this young Rabbi? A hometown boy? A Sabbath-keeper? A teacher sent from God?

They were mesmerized by his teaching. "This man speaks as one who knows the truth personally, instead of merely quoting the opinions of others as our rabbis do." Jesus was confirming his identity—answering the question on everyone's mind—who is this Galilean?

Life Applications

We Are Never Alone

An opioid drug crises is claiming thousands of lives. Road rage killings are almost commonplace. Mass murders with military style assault rifles, killings at schools, workplaces, playgrounds, in movies, at concerts, and sporting events have people on edge. Authorities are finding a common thread in many of the killers' profiles: ordinary seeming persons who quietly become mentally unstable, alienated from society, subjected to bullying, or otherwise shunned or feeling disrespected. Even more tragic is they seal themselves off from people who could come to their aid and rescue them. They often confide in no one but keep their issues bottled up inside until something snaps. It's almost impossible for authorities to detect and deter them until a tragedy explodes. A lone wolf is a policeman's nightmare and Satan's pawn. There is a better way. God has surrounded us with people to help.

Nineteen-year-old Johnny Agar finished his 5K race, despite cerebral palsy which makes physical activity exceedingly difficult. What convinced Johnny to push past his limit and try the impossible? He and his dad, Jeff, have teamed up to compete in many races—with Dad pushing and Johnny riding. But this particular day, Johnny wanted to finish the race by himself. So, halfway through their competition, Dad took him out of his cart, helped him to his walker, and followed Johnny as he completed the race on his own two feet. Family and friends were yelling encouragement, cheering him on, and celebrating his remarkable achievement. "It made it easier for me to do it with them behind me," Johnny told a reporter. "Their encouragement is what drove me."

For reflection:
Are you by personality an introvert, preferring not to share your problems?
Why is it unwise to refuse help when you feel overwhelmed?

When Not to Negotiate

Mahatma Gandhi refused to accept unfair treatment of his fellowman. Renouncing violence, he organized his fellow citizens to protest their abuse by boycotts and other peaceful means. As a result, millions of hopeless people gained their freedom and the independent nation of India was born.

When John Lewis was 23-years-old, he joined the now-famous "March on Washington D.C." led by Dr. Martin Luther King Jr. to secure civil rights for black people. Asked by journalist Bill Moyers fifty years later, how he was affected by Dr. Kings' "I Have a Dream" speech, Lewis, now a U.S. Congressman, replied, "You couldn't leave after hearing him speak and go back to business as usual. You had to do something, you had to act."

For reflection:
Can you point to other examples where Jesus
refused to go along to get along?
When have you faced such a decision? How did you respond?

Go and Tell

The gospel was being confirmed by mighty signs and wonders. The good news Jesus was bringing to the people was enthusiastically welcomed. Still is. Here's the story of an innocent child once captured by demons of darkness:

My name is Anne Marie Grana. I was born in Lima, Peru into a wealthy family; my cradle was made, literally, from gold. My mom and I were best friends, especially after her divorce.

However, one day I was forced to leave my house because her divorce and alcoholism had left my mother inescapably confused. I was 14 years old and had no idea how to survive on the streets. I found "friends" who introduced me to drugs. When I had no money, I stole things to get more drugs. This lifestyle brought me to the dark streets of the city, and I became pregnant. My son's father became a cocaine user.

When my child was born my mother and grandfather came to the hospital and took me home with them. I wanted so badly to quit drugs but again fell into addiction. They threw me back onto the streets, and this time was even worse. I got involved with narcotics dealers and dangerous criminals. I went to jail for assault and robbery. My story was in the newspapers and magazines: "Ex-Miss Peru involved in assault and robbery.... prosecutors asking for 10 years of prison time."

It was in that horrible prison, in my desperation and loneliness, that God touched me with his love. One day I was walking through the prison halls and heard people singing praises. I walked into the room, and someone gave me a bible and told me to read Psalm 27:10: "When my father and mother forsake me, then the Lord will take me up."

The words entered my heart. I could not stop crying. I needed to hear this, needed a touch from God. I realized I was a sinner, yet God loved me. That day I accepted Jesus as my Lord and Savior. My circumstances didn't matter anymore; I had peace with God.

I was sentenced to seven years of prison. One day God spoke to me as I was reading his Word: "I will go before you and will level the mountains: I will break down gates of bronze and cut through bars of iron." (Isaiah 45:2).

I asked, "How will you do it, Lord?" A few days later I received the answer. It arrived in an official envelope from the President of Peru. It was a pardon for me! God was doing what he had promised me. I was instantly freed from the dual-yoked slavery of sin and prison!"

Anne Marie went to Bogota, Columbia for two years to study missions, then came to the United States as a missionary, where she survived surgeries for brain cancer and lung cancer. Finally, she returned to Peru where she shares her story with drug addicts, abused women, and others caught up on the same dark streets that once enslaved her. People are waiting to hear it, receive it, and be redeemed.

For reflection:
What is an ambassador's responsibility (e.g., to represent a higher authority, conduct business, relay messages)?
How are you fulfilling your role as God's ambassador?

JESUS STOPS A STORM

(Gospel account in Matthew 8:18-27; Mark 4: 35-41; Luke 8:22-25)

After teaching in the temple, Jesus said to his disciples, "Let's cross to the other side of the lake."

As evening came, they started across the Sea of Galilee. Suddenly, a fierce storm arose, and high waves began breaking into their boat. Jesus was sleeping. Frantically, they woke him up, shouting, "Teacher, don't you even care that we're about to drown?"

Once awake, he rebuked the wind and said to the waves, "Quiet down!" The wind suddenly stopped, and a great calm settled over the water. Then, Jesus asked them, "Why are you so afraid? Do you still not have faith in me?"

It sounds like a strange question—after all, these fishermen knew storms could be fatal. But Jesus had said, "Let's cross over to the other side of the lake." He didn't say, "Let's try to get across if the storm doesn't swamp the boat."

They were filled with awe, whispering among themselves, "Who is this that even the winds and sea obey him?"

Background

The disciples were powerfully attracted to Jesus as a charismatic rabbi and friend. So much so, they were willing to forsake their fishing nets and "day jobs" to follow him. Yet, they were only beginning to vaguely understand that their beloved companion was far more than a gifted personality.

A few moments after they crawled in the boat with him, they witnessed something no words would suffice to explain—and their faith was gloriously stretched. They would need to be tough to survive in a godless society which hated Christ for exposing their dark ways. Also, they needed this near-death encounter to test their faith in the keeping power of Jesus. They failed miserably, but their teacher used this terrifying moment to remind them they could trust him.

The disciples were being schooled in the wars of fear. They had Jesus in their boat. They were being reminded—not so gently—how important it is to be traveling with God. People without God have reason to fear—they're aboard a sinking ship.

When the scared-out-of-their-wits disciples finally awakened Jesus, he sat up, rubbed his eyes, yawned, and asked, "What's the problem, guys?" (Free translation.)

This episode needs no elaboration. The disciples were being taught Theology 101. Try to imagine their eyes bugging out when it actually happened—suddenly the wind died down and the waves became glass. The world has seen an untold number of so-called "Messiahs" come and go. How many of them do you suppose have stopped a storm?

After their hearts slowed down and they had regained their wits, the disciples began shaking their heads, asking each other, "Did you see what I saw—who is this man that even the wind and waves obey him?"

It's a reasonable question. By the way, the answer was beautifully written on the back of a golf card in 1951 by American songwriter Johnny Lange: *"Who made the mountain, who made the tree, who made the river flow into the sea? And who hung the moon in the starry sky? Someone bigger than you and I."*

Good question, obvious answer.

The disciples mistook Jesus sleeping through the storm as indifference. "Master, don't you care if we all drown?" How could Jesus sleep through such a harrowing nightmare?

We know he was devoted to pre-dawn prayer. He was Spirit-filled. He and his Father were always in sweet accord. He was tired, needing to rest before continuing his kingdom work. His Father knew this and apparently gave him assurance that he did not need to be "on duty and in control" every moment.

Obviously, Jesus was depending on our heavenly Father to protect him. Trusting like a little child, he laid his head on a pillow and entered into blissful sleep. Do you know anyone whose faith is so solidly grounded they can sleep through storms?

Life Applications

Storms Help Us Grow

When I was in college, I veered from the straight path and was not honoring God. I was still close enough to our family farm to go home on weekends to help my preacher dad on the farm. On those times alone with him, Dad would gently remind me of what I'd been taught, what I had believed, and that God chastens every disobedient child. Dad's love would not let me go. In fact, his "woodshed sermons" were making me downright uncomfortable.

One Sunday afternoon, as I was driving back to the dormitory, the sky grew dark, the wind began howling, and a frightening electrical storm struck. I was sure a tornado was about to strike. I pulled over to the curb, stopped the engine, moved oved to the middle of the car, waited, and began praying. Lightening was crashing all around me, and I fully expected the car to take a direct hit. This lasted for what seemed an eternity. Finally, the storm passed, and I drove on back, shaking like a leaf. I couldn't help wondering if Dad had asked the Lord to give him a little help! Finally, God had my full attention.

The Bible says the Lord tests his chosen ones. So, if you're a believer, get ready! Jesus was preparing his disciples for a life-long journey of hard knocks.

For reflection:
What storm(s) has God taken you through?
How has overcoming difficulties helped you grow?

Who's in Your Boat?

Pastor Dale O'Shields climbed up on an outside extension ladder to clean his gutters. Without warning, the ladder shifted, and he found himself clinging to it from a high altitude. He was hanging in such an awkward position that the fall could be fatal or break his back or neck.

Suddenly in free fall, the ladder stopped for a second in mid-air—"just long enough for me to shift my position on the ladder so that my vital organs were not so vulnerable." He hit the hard ground rolling and was not seriously injured. There was no wind or earthly reason for the ladder to pause in mid-air.

When he tells the story now after many years, he's still in awe. He was not alone. For a moment, God joined him on the ladder.

For reflection:
When a storm breaks upon you unexpectedly, who will be in your frail vessel? (If it's the Master of wind and waves, what have you to fear?)

Responding to a Crisis

Catherine Marshall, wife of the famous Senate Chaplain Peter Marshall, loved praying for anyone in need. One day she received a call from an Episcopal priest about Danny, the 5-month-old son of a young couple in his church. Danny had been in a Miami hospital since birth. Only eleven pounds, he was unable to breath outside his oxygen tent. The parents feared that lack of oxygen may have damaged his brain and destroyed his eyesight.

The parents were believers and had come to their priest seeking help. He began praying for little Danny but to no avail. He remembered Catherine Marshall's prayer ministry and called her one day to ask her advice.

"Have you anointed the baby with oil and laid hands on him as you prayed?" she asked. The priest thanked her and immediately went to the hospital with the baby's mother and gave him unction for healing.

Six weeks later Catherine received great news. "I'm delighted to tell you that little Danny is doing marvelously" (*The Helper* by Catherine Marshall, 1978).

For reflection:
How do you normally respond in a crisis?
What is the implication of Jesus
"rebuking the wind and stopping the storm"?

PETER'S MOTHER-IN-LAW

(Gospel account in Matthew 8:14-17; Mark 1:29-34; Luke 4:38-41)

Jesus left the synagogue and went home with Peter and Andrew, accompanied also by James and John. They found Peter's mother-in-law lying in bed with a high fever, so they asked Jesus to heal her. He went to her bed, bent over her, and rebuked the fever. The fever left her. Jesus took her hand and helped her up. At once, she began to wait on them.

Peter and Jesus were already beginning to realize how much they loved each other and how their lives were to be forever linked. Lifelong friends are a special blessing from God and one of the ways he shows us how much he loves us, another sparkling gem in the abundant life. Jesus' special bond with Peter shows us his humanity in a warm, glowing light. It also reminds us how important it is to spend time with those we treasure.

We don't know if Peter asked Jesus to come home with him to heal his mother-in-law, but it's not unlikely. Was Jesus a busy man? Of course, but what's more important than a friend in need? The Lord was developing a special love for the big fisherman. If Peter was hurting, Jesus was feeling his pain.

The disciples had unknowingly enrolled in spiritual boot camp. Their next three years with Jesus would be intense. In his brief time with them, however, he would not let spiritual lessons eclipse their duty to respond to human needs.

Background

Do you still remember how excited you were when your parents decided you were old enough to stay overnight at a friend's house? That was a big deal! You no doubt had other childhood friends, but not all of them were so special you wanted to spend the night at their house. Do you have one or more of these God-given special friends now? Are you allowing yourself time to enjoy them?

We don't even know Peter's mother-in-law's name. Yet, her story lives forever. Another nameless soul who captured the world's imagination, she gives us one solitary clue to her identity. She was so eager to get back to work, she almost jumped out of bed! She apparently found her place of ministry in homemaking, cooking, and serving her family and their guests. Someone said of this story, "How terrible that these grown men would allow this poor convalescing woman to get up and begin serving them! They should have been waiting on her." This critic was appalled at what she perceived to be the men's chauvinism.

When Jesus spoke to this woman's fever, it was not to charm but to eradicate it. About Jesus' voice, Khalil Gibran (*Jesus, the Son of Man*) wrote, "When Jesus spoke the whole world hushed to listen. He spoke to the sea... He spoke to the mountain...and He spoke to the angels beyond the mountain. The sound of his voice was like cool water in a land of drought... And still his speech slumbers within our breast like a love-song half forgotten, and sometimes it burns through to our memory."

From *Psalm* 29:
The glorious Lord thunders and his voice echoes over the ocean.
The voice of the Lord booms over the waters;
His voice is heard in all its might and glory.
It breaks the great cedars and makes mountains jump like calves.
The voice of the Lord shakes the mighty oaks and strips off their leaves;
While everyone in his Temple shouts, "Glory to God!"

Peter's mother-in-law received far more than a physical healing that day. She experienced an up-close encounter with God.

The *Gospel of John* tells us more than she could have possibly known about Jesus: that he and the Father were together in the beginning. Christ was called the Word. The Word was with God, and the Word was God. Through him all things were made; without him nothing was made that has been made. In him was life, and that life was the light of all mankind. (Passages from John 1, paraphrased)

Life Applications

The Voice

Sid Roth attended synagogue and trained for his bar mitzvah before discovering the Messiah. Since then, Sid has investigated the supernatural for four decades. His television program, "It's Supernatural," documents everyday miracles around the world. In his bestseller, *They Thought for Themselves,* Sid tells of ten amazing Jews God spoke to in personally unique but unmistakable ways. One was an atheist, another a Holocaust survivor, one was a multi-millionaire, another a media executive, and still another a Ph.D.. What did they all have in common? They heard God calling—and they thought for themselves. Their conclusion: Jesus is the true Yushua who for thousands of years God had been promising to their ancestors.

Indeed, God's voice is still ringing true to all who will listen.

For reflection:
When have you heard the Lord speaking to you? How?
Through what mechanism(s)?

When God Becomes Personal

This same God became personal for Safaa Ibraham, an Egyptian immigrant to the United States. She claimed Dot and me as her "adopted parents" when she met us through a home Bible study and we took an interest in her—and so we got to her know her and her story.

Safaa was born into a Muslim family. Her friends were Muslim. Her community and nation are 90 percent Muslim. Safaa grew up with a deep spiritual yearning but an empty heart. This is her story in her own words:

"All this time, my soul was fainting with longing for the True God and his salvation. The Holy Spirit began drawing me to Him. Looking back, I now see that Jesus Christ, himself, King of the universe, had sought me out and found me.

One night in a dream I heard a Voice saying, "Utter the name of Jesus, and this problem will be solved." The problem I was focusing on was my troubled marriage. When I awoke the next morning, I said to myself, "What can the name of Jesus do for me? There's no solution to my problem, but, I want to know more about this Jesus." So, I went to a bookstore and found a book, *Interview with Jesus across Time.* As I raced through the pages, I was flooded with joy, knowing this was the One I'd been yearning for. So, I asked the Lord to give me another sign.

He gave me a second dream in which I saw a window filled with beautiful rings. I could not decide which one I liked best, but my sister, who was standing beside me, took one of the rings and put it on my finger. I looked at it and saw Jesus' face engraved on the front of it. I felt a peace like never before in my life and told my sister, "Yes, this one's for me."

I awoke and knew this was the sign I'd asked God for. I sought out a church and visited it the following Sunday. After the service I told the pastor, "I love Jesus and want to be baptized."

He replied, "That's not the way it usually happens. We normally have to seek out those needing the Lord, but you sought us out."

I told him my story and was baptized on September 13, 1992, my birthday!

Since that glorious day, I have been enjoying the presence of the Lord—in awe of the mighty miracles he has done in my life. I'm so thrilled to know God first loved me and called me, sought me out, found me, and redeemed me. It was meant to be. My heart is his for eternity, hallelujah!"

Sadly, since she converted from Islam, Safaa cannot safely return to Egypt to see her beloved family. Yet, she refuses to conceal her faith. She will never deny what Christ has done for her by becoming a "secret believer".

For reflection:

Can you pinpoint a time God became personal to you? (Was it a sudden revelation, a gradual but growing understanding, or in some other way?)

Responding to God's Love With Service and Humility

Jade Chang is said by her friends to be the world's greatest cook. She's one of those quiet servants with the gift of hospitality. Often, she has enlisted the help of her husband George and her family to prepare a special banquet for her whole church. When word gets out that Jade is preparing a meal, church attendance improves remarkably! She never wants to be in the spotlight, preferring simply to bless people with her food and friendship. You will not see Jade on the TV food channels—and that's fine with her friends. We cherish her loving spirit of giving, so much like the love, humility, and servant orientation of Peter's mother-in-law, and are delighted to accept it on her terms.

For reflection:

Are you willing to be anonymous—a quiet, cheerful, generous giver?

TEN LEPERS HEALED

(Gospel account in Luke 17:11-19)

Jesus pushed on toward Jerusalem, coming to the border between Galilee and Samaria. As he entered a village there, he was met by ten men suffering from leprosy, a dreaded skin disease.

They stood at a distance, shouting, "Jesus, Master, have mercy on us!"

Jesus looked at them and said, "Go, and let the priests examine you." And as they went, their leprosy disappeared.

One of the ten, when he saw that he was healed, came back to Jesus, shouting, "I'm healed!" He fell face down on the ground at the feet of Jesus, thanking him. The gospel writer seemed amazed to report, "This man who returned was a Samaritan."

Jesus was pleased but also curious. "Didn't I heal ten men? Where are the other nine? Does only this foreigner give glory to God?" And Jesus said to the man, "Arise, go thy way: thy faith has made thee whole." (Luke 17:19 KJV)

Background

In that day, leprosy was a death sentence. Victims suffered agony as their skin, then their fingers and toes, then hands and feet, and finally their internal organs rotted away. The disease was a humiliating, disfiguring, dignity-robbing way to die. Possibly the ultimate humiliation and loss came when they were banished from family, friends, and their fellow humans. Lepers were forbidden to touch or approach those not infected. The best society could do was banish them into leper colonies and hope for saints of mercy to come tend to their sores, feed, and care for them. The disease was so totally isolating that broken hearts and loneliness could cause more pain than their wounds.

Yet, these lepers had heard of Jesus—likely the great miracles he was doing—and they believed he had the power to heal them. They clung to a slim thread of hope—that Jesus wouldn't reject them. Yes, they were aware no medicine or treatment yet existed to heal them. Still, they had not totally resigned themselves to their fate. Deep in their innermost beings, they knew that nothing is impossible with God. And at just the right time, Jesus passed by.

Did you notice how cautiously the lepers approached Jesus? They stood pitifully at a distance, crying out to him. Being highly contagious, they had no choice. They were quarantined by law—forbidden to embrace anyone or touch them. A life sentence of isolation, a tragic future.

Jesus didn't hesitate when the lepers pleaded for mercy. He didn't interview each one to document their mistakes and transgressions. Notice Jesus didn't say, "Okay, you've been healed." Instead, he gave the lepers their marching orders.

"Go show yourself to the priests." That was their part so they departed quickly in joy and anticipation.

We don't know what happened to the other nine lepers who were healed. Did their disease return? How did they respond when people asked them how they were healed? Did they believe and become Christians? The Bible is silent.

What we do know is this: they missed a golden opportunity to give glory to God by returning to thank Jesus for their delivery, for restoring their dreams, for giving them a new life. Jesus was pleased to see even one, a foreigner, returning to give glory to God. If we only realized how greatly it pleases our Lord, surely we would more faithfully acknowledge our blessings.

In quiet times with God, how refreshing it is to sometimes lay aside our petitions and begin singing his praises, to launch out on a river of joy, giving glory to God. Counting our blessings is one of the highest forms of worship.

Has God been gracious to you? Has he blessed your family? Protected you from harm, danger, and evil? Given you opportunities to honor him and bless others? When you lavish gifts on your loved ones, do you expect and appreciate a word of thanks?

"God has no grandchildren!" is a popular way of saying each of us is accountable to God. We're not saved by Grandmother's faith. Her love and prayers may bring us to the cross, but it's our feet carrying us there—and our knees that bow down. It's your heart that believes and your tongue that confesses.

The good news is—just as God doesn't automatically save us because of someone else's faith—he doesn't brand people or disqualify them. People will surprise you. It was the despised Samaritan who came back, not God's chosen ones. Our world today is fractured by fear, anger, and hatred. We separate ourselves from foreigners, those of differing skin color, political parties, and religions. You can imagine God looking down on our petty bickering, shaking his head, saying sadly, "There they go again!" Have you been touched by the lovingkindness of our heavenly Father?

Life Applications

People at a Distance, Take Heart!

The psalmist said, "I waited patiently for the Lord. Then, he heard my prayers. He reached down and took hold of me and lifted me out of the mud and mire." The songwriter put it beautifully:

"He lifted me up from the miry clay
He put my feet on a rock to stay.
His precious blood washed my sins away
He lifted me up, up, up, he lifted me up!" (Author unknown)

A young lady shared this story with her church class: "I grew up in a dysfunctional family where God was used to threaten us if we misbehaved. We knew nothing of his love. I became convinced that God was going to kill me—because, of course, I was sinning. I actually felt like I should wear rubber sole shoes in case God decided to strike me with lightning! When I heard the gospel for the first time, I was blown away to learn Jesus loves me, wants the best for me, and even died for me. What a relief to live in love instead of cringing in fear!"

For reflection:
What keeps you at a distance from God? What can you do about it—or what can you ask/allow God to do about it?

Jesus Offers Both Healing and Wholeness

Pastor Jentzel Franklin, in a telecast of his Kingdom Connection program, noted that, "All ten were healed by Jesus but only one was pronounced "whole".

Those healed had likely lost fingers and toes, even feet, ears, and noses, causing terrible disfigurement. Their disease was stopped and eradicated, but they may have been left with its tragic aftermath. If so, imagine their struggles trying to regain acceptance back into a fearful society. But, the Lord left no doubt that the one who came back giving glory to God was made whole.

The medical profession has only recently come to the reality of holistic healing, recognizing that a person's health is influenced by physical, mental, physiological, and spiritual factors. What doctors have been missing for so many years, Jesus was practicing two thousand years ago!

For reflection:
Would you settle for physical healing when God offers spiritual wholeness?

A Thankful Heart Honors God

"When I was a child, my family lived in a house my father built in the cedar breaks west of Ducanville, Texas. Our house had a small kitchen-dinette area, two bedrooms, and a great room with a large stone fireplace. That fireplace was the center of warmth in our home. There were five people in our family. Since we had only two bedrooms, I slept year-round on a porch with canvas screens that rolled down to the floor. Summers were delightful; winters were cold.

I remember dashing from the warmth of the living room onto the porch, tiptoeing across the frost-covered plank floor in my bare feet, leaping into bed and burrowing under a great mountain of blankets. Then, when hail, sleet, or snow lashed our house and wind howled through the eaves like a pack of wolves, I snuggled down in sheltered rest. "Snug as a bug in a rug," my mother used to say. I doubt that any child ever felt so warm and secure."

Even as a young child, David was thankful to be protected from those icy Texas winters, but his story doesn't end there. "Now I know the greatest security of all: God Himself. I can "lie down in peace and sleep" (Ps. 4-8), knowing that He is my shelter from the stinging storms of life." (*Our Daily Bread*, 2014)

For reflection:
When has God blessed you but you forgot to thank him? (Take heart: It's better late than never!)

MAN WITH A SHRIVELED HAND

(Gospel account in Matthew 12:9-15; Mark 3: 1-6; Luke 6: 5 -11)

Jesus went into a synagogue, where he encountered a man with a shriveled hand. The Pharisees were looking for a reason to accuse Christ of breaking the law so they watched closely to see if he would heal the man on the Sabbath. The Lord read their minds and knew they were trying to trap him. Ignoring the danger, he said to the man with the deformed hand, "Stand up and come here to the front so everybody can see you."

The man came forward and stood there waiting. Then Jesus said to his critics, "I have a question for you. Is it legal to do good deeds on the Sabbath, or is it a day for doing harm?" Silence.

As his accusers strained to see, Jesus' penetrating eyes scalded them with anger. Then, he said to the man with the paralyzed hand, "Reach out your hand." He did so, and it was completely restored, just as sound as the other one.

BACKGROUND

On this day of destiny, Jesus was in God's house, teaching and fellowshipping with the people. In the middle of his message, Jesus noticed a man whose arm had withered and was hanging limp at his side. In rural and rustic Palestine, people worked with their hands—farming, fishing, and carpentering. It was an agrarian culture where men earned their bread by the sweat of their brow and strength of their hands.

Jesus put aside his sermon, as the Holy Spirit directed his eyes and spoke clearly to his heart to restore this crippled pilgrim. Here we catch a glimpse into God's mindset: Jesus noticed the man—and his deformity momentarily eclipsed his Sabbath message. If we're following Jesus, our hearts will be attuned to helping one another.

Jesus knew he was putting his own life in danger by ignoring one of the rigid Jewish religious laws. He also knew this man had suffered enough. It was a no-brainer for Jesus. Would he be intimidated by evil hypocrites, or would he follow the prompting of the Holy Spirit? He knew what he must do, and he did it gladly and fearlessly.

Jesus knew his time here on earth would be short. The forces of darkness would have their day. It was only a matter of time. These forces would fabricate charges against him. False witnesses would lie, he would be convicted in mock trials—and pay with his life.

Yet while it was still day, our Lord knew he must do his Father's work. So, he didn't hesitate to cure this man—while his future killers watched and waited.

He knew the religious big shots were burning with jealousy, fearful they were losing power to this unschooled Rabbi. They were looking for an excuse to accuse Jesus and get rid of him. They had blood in their eyes and murder in their hearts. But Jesus knew what they were thinking.

If they were hoping to intimidate Jesus with their cloak-and-dagger threats, they failed. Our Lord knew he had come from the Father and would soon be returning to him. Meanwhile, he had a charge to keep.

His charge to us is backed by his faithfulness. Here's a watchword: Keep doing your good kingdom work, depending, trusting, and praying: "Father, thy will be done. Deliver us from evil."

The gospel of Mark tells us that Jesus looked around at them in anger, deeply distressed at their stubborn hearts. Yet, he was not going to let these wolves in sheep's clothing dictate his life. He knew what he must do and he did it.

Ecclesiastes tells us there's a time and season for all things. A time to be quiet and a time to speak. Jesus decided to speak out and expose the wicked religious bigots.

Jesus knew the risk he was taking: He could be arrested for breaking the Sabbath. His own people (the religious authorities) were plotting with their Roman occupiers to kill him without inciting a riot.

So, he challenged them in front of the people: "If any of you has a sheep and it falls into a pit on the Sabbath, will you not take hold of it and lift it out? How much more valuable is a man than a sheep!"

Then, Jesus said to them, "I ask you, which is lawful on the Sabbath: to do good or to do evil, to save life or destroy it?" But they remained silent.

Clearly, Jesus wasn't asking these questions because he didn't know the answers. He wanted people to see the midnight-black hearts lurking under the Pharisees' holy robes. Someone said of the Holocaust, "The only thing required for evil to succeed is for good men to do nothing."

Life Applications

Following God's Priority

As Christians, we're subject to the law. We're taught to respect and obey authority. Yet, we may face situations where we must decide between following an unjust law or God's higher law. And, as Jesus did, we must follow God's will—even if we suffer for doing so.

When God calls a man or woman into foreign missions, they must make a conscious decision to lay their lives on the line. Among many unreached people, spiritual forces of darkness violently oppose the gospel, afraid of losing their powers over the people. Mission and charity workers are in danger every day—and their families. In some cases, the violence becomes so dangerous, they have to abandon their homes and try to escape with their lives.

Take a look at the category of "murdered missionaries" in Wikipedia. You will find 89 pages of people who over time, including today, have been killed while serving God. In 1980 in one of the better-known instances of murdered missionaries, five members of the National Guard in El Salvador raped and murdered three Maryknoll nuns, Maura Clarke, Ita Ford, and Ursuline Dorothy Kasel, and one lay missionary, Jean Donova. Last year (2017) dozens of servants of God were murdered, including Coptic priest Samaan Shebata, hacked to death in the streets of Cairo, Baptist minister Ange-Apoléon Ngakolada, target of Muslims in the Central African Republic for the church he built there, and Sudanese church leader Younan Abdulla, stabbed while taking part in a peaceful protest against the government. And, should anyone think that these kinds of murders take place only in countries at war or in poverty, missionaries in the United States have also been killed.

For reflection:
Are you following God's plans for your life?
What adjustments would you need to make to do so?
Would you follow it if it caused you to suffer or put your life in jeopardy?

Cooperating With God

John was a rebellious teenager, grieving his mother and father by using and dealing drugs. On a weekend family trip to Virginia Beach, they allowed John to bring a friend along for companionship. The boys stayed out nights, drugging and drinking, then sleeping it off the next day. On their last night before returning home, his parents insisted John and his friend come home at 10 p.m. and be ready to leave the next morning. Midnight came, and they were not home. His father went driving around the beach looking for the boys, finally appealing to the police for help. When finally located, the boys were talking to a Christian outreach group involved in beach ministry. John had accepted the gospel; his friend was also convinced but not willing to make such a life-changing decision. Two weeks later, John's friend and a companion were in a motorcycle collision that took his life. He had believed the message of salvation but lost forever the opportunity to turn from his sin and follow Jesus.

For reflection:
Are you following God's plans for your life?
What adjustments would you need to make to do so?

Confronting Evil

Survivors of the Holocaust, are still telling stories of good people risking their lives to hide and protect Jews from Nazi mass murderers and their unspeakable gas chambers. Such heroes have been immortalized by books and movies including *The Hiding Place* by Corrie Ten Boom and *Schindler's List* by Tom Keneal. When these brave souls were caught, they often suffered the same fate as those they died to protect. Thankfully, even in the black midnight of Hitler's Germany, Jesus was still passing by, inspiring men, women, and families of great courage to step forward, including less-celebrated ones like Sofka Skipwith, a Russian princess who helped rescue Jews while she herself was imprisoned in France; Klara Baic, a Serbian single mother who sheltered two Jewish boys in her home; Mother Superior Maria Agnese Tribbioli, who hid Jewish families in her convent in Florence during German raids; Lois Gunden, a Mennonite from Indiana who rescued Jewish children in France; Joseph Migneret, a French school principal who rescued Jewish students in his school; Benjamin, Blankenstein, a Dutch school teacher who rescued a Jewish family and paid with his life; and Johann Westerweel, another Dutch teacher who also paid with his life when he established a rescue network.

For reflection:
Has personal risk kept you from confronting evil?
Does Jesus promise to be with us always embolden you?

*A PARALYZED MAN–
FORGIVEN & HEALED*

(Gospel account in Matthew 9:1-8; Mark 2:1-13; Luke 5:17-26)

Jesus returned to Capernaum, and the news of his arrival spread quickly. Soon the house where he was staying was so packed with visitors there wasn't room for one more person, not even outside the door. And he preached the Word to them.

Four men arrived bearing a paralyzed man on a stretcher. They struggled to get him through the crowd to Jesus. Failing to push through, they carried the man up onto the roof, removed some clay tiles, and lowered the sick man down, smack in front of Jesus! Jesus first told the invalid his sins were forgiven, then healed him as the crowd watched.

Background

In this story, don't overlook the tenderhearted men carrying the stretcher. How far are you inclined to go to help others? For most of us, it doesn't come naturally.

The Lord's primary mission is highlighted in this story. He came to preach good news to the poor—to set captives free, to proclaim the year of God's favor. We're needy people—needful of food, clothing, shelter, medical care, and healing. Yet deeper still are our spiritual needs. God's wandering children need to be reconciled to our Creator. How desperately they need to hear his invitation to eternal life. The life application for us is clear: Lost sheep will never find Jesus unless someone guides them.

Does sharing your faith come natural to you? Think of some less intimidating ways to do so, such as organizing sports activities, movie nights, cook-outs, or game nights. Be creative, get people talking about what's going on in their lives.

The man's faith, and that of his friends, drew the Lord's attention. Faith was placing the sick man in line for his miracle. You can take it to the bank: faith always draws God's attention.

When Jesus told the man, "My son, your sins are forgiven." The religious pooh-bahs threw a fit.

"Who does this man think he is? This is blasphemy! Who but God can forgive sin?" they began muttering to themselves.

Immediately Jesus knew in his spirit what they were thinking in their hearts, and said to them, "Why do you think this is blasphemy? Is it easier to say to this paralyzed man, 'Your sins are forgiven' or 'Get up, pick up your mat and walk?'

I will prove that I, the Son of Man, have authority on earth to forgive sins."

Then Jesus turned to the paralyzed man and said, "Stand up, take your mat, and go on home, because you are healed!"

The religious pretenders had stumbled upon the truth—only God has the power to forgive sin—yet they refused to believe their own eyes.

Life Applications

Am I the Real Deal?

The paralyzed man in this story had the kind of friends we dream of becoming. We may desperately need such friends ourselves one day. Would you have volunteered to carry the stretcher?

Matthew Kelly in his powerful devotional book, *Rediscover Jesus*, tells of a business team rushing to a New York airport to catch their flight home. As they bolted toward a cab, yelling to get the driver's attention, they knocked over a small produce stand. The others kept running, but Paul stopped and went back to help. From the taxi, the others called out to Paul, "Come on, you'll miss your flight."

"Go ahead without me," Paul told them as he made his way back across the street to the sidewalk covered with produce. At that moment, he realized the woman behind the stand was blind. She was just standing there crying softly with tears running down her face.

"It's okay; it's okay," Paul said to her as he got down on his hands and knees and began picking up the fruit and vegetables. He sorted out the damaged produce and put all the rest back up on the stand. Then, he turned to the woman and asked, "Are you okay?"

She nodded through her tears. Then, reaching for his wallet, Paul took out some bills and passed them to her, saying, "This money should cover the damages."

With that, Paul turned and began walking away.

"Mister," the woman called after him. Paul paused and turned around. "Are you Jesus?"

"Oh, no," he replied.

The woman nodded and continued, "I only ask because I prayed for Jesus to help me as I heard my fruit falling all over the sidewalk."

Interesting question, don't you think? And Paul was right to quickly deny it. "To you and to you alone, O God, be the glory!" the psalmist sang.

But the fruit stand lady had sensed something in Paul's heart. She could make a convincing argument that *Jesus is still passing by.*

For reflection:
How can I know if I'm the real deal?
How much are you willing to be inconvenienced to help others?

Faith Gets God's Attention

Depending solely on God's provision, English evangelist George Mueller created homes for more than 10,000 orphans and established 117 schools caring for 120,000 children. All this he accomplished entirely by hard work and fervent unceasing prayer; making no appeals for financial support. He never went into debt but believed that God would supply everything his charges needed. And God answered Muller's utter dependence on Him. Sometimes when he was penniless and the children were without food, donations miraculously came hours before they were needed to feed the children. By his incredible faith that God answers the prayers of his servants, George Mueller preached the gospel, taught, fed and educated thousands.

For reflection:
What "great things" do you need God to do in your life? (For your family and friends, your church, your work place, your nation?)

Questions About His Divinity

Imagine yourself as an eyewitness. You saw this terribly handicapped man being lowered on a stretcher. You heard the words Jesus spoke. You saw the man jump up and go home on his new feet. What would you conclude? Would you want to praise or kill him?

H.B. Garlock was a missionary pioneer to western Africa, penetrating where no white man had gone, bringing the gospel to fierce warriors and head-hunters. One day Garlock was surrounded by an angry tribe of cannibals. Their witch doctor threw his wand on the ground before Garlock as if to say, "Before we kill and eat you, you're permitted to speak." Garlock remembered Jesus' words in Mark 13:11: "Don't worry beforehand about what you will speak, but whatever is given you in that hour, speak that; for it is not you who speak, but the Holy Spirit." He opened his mouth and a flood of words came out that he had never learned. When he finished, the witch doctor asked for forgiveness on behalf of the tribe for trying to harm him. Garlock could only marvel at the power of the Christ he was preaching.

For reflection:
What do you think was blinding his opponents?
How does one "harden his heart" against God?

FEEDING THE FIVE THOUSAND

(Gospel account in Matthew 14:13-23; Mark 6:30-46; Luke 9:10-17; John 6:1-15)

Because so many people were pressing in upon them, Jesus and his disciples did not even have a chance to eat. So, he said to them, "Come with me to a quiet place and let's get some rest." They went away by themselves in a boat to a solitary place, but many saw them leaving, ran on foot from nearby towns, and got there ahead of them. When Jesus landed, he saw the large crowd. His heart went out to them, and he healed their sick.

When the crowd following him grew hungry, he took five loaves of barley bread and two small fish, gave thanks to God, and had them passed out to the people. The number of men who ate was about 5,000, not counting women and children.

Background

The Holy Spirit filled Jesus with power from on high. Despite his own hunger and fatigue, he waded into the crowd and began healing the sick and teaching.

As evening approached, the disciples came to him and said, "This is a remote place and it's already getting late. Send the crowds away so they can go to the villages and buy themselves some food."

Jesus replied. "They don't need to go away. You give them something to eat."

Never buy into the idea that God, after creating the world, put it on automatic pilot or retreated back to heaven to sit under an oscillating fan, sipping iced tea. No, our heavenly Father knows, cares, and gets involved to sustain and care for you. He never turns a blind eye to his children.

Andrew, Simon Peter's brother, spoke up, "Here's a boy with five small barley loaves and two fish—but how far will they go?"

The logistics didn't add up. How could five thousand hungry men share two hand-sized fish and five brick-sized loaves of bread?

"Have the people sit down." Jesus told the disciples. Apparently he wasn't looking at the impossibility—he had something greater in mind.

Don't miss this part: Taking the five loaves and two fish, Jesus looked up into heaven and gave thanks. He was acknowledging what God had already supplied—and asking for more.

After giving thanks, Jesus broke the loaves and gave them to the disciples to set before the people. He did the same with the fish. They all ate until they were satisfied. Then, he said to his disciples, "Gather the pieces that are left over. Let nothing be wasted." So, they gathered them and filled twelve baskets with the left-overs. Talk about doggie-bags!

Life Applications

God Cares About all Your Needs

What does this tender story signify for us? God cares deeply for his people. He feels our pain—be it hunger, sickness, loneliness or confusion. Jesus ignored his own needs to help them. God numbers the hairs on your head. He knows and cares about anything touching your life.

The Christian Embassy has a unique mission in the nation's capital, ministering to senators, representatives, and their professional staff. (Someone's going to say, Thank God!) A small cadre works to establish one on one contact with the people who make our laws and discharge the nation's business. Their goal is to represent Christ in this pressure-cooker environment by ministering to the spiritual needs of our political leaders. They arrange for outstanding Christian celebrities to speak, bringing their personal testimony of how the Lord changed their lives for the better. Imagine that, God even cares about your Congressman!

For reflection:
What does it do for you to realize God cares about all your needs?
How does this affect your response to others?

God Multiplies What We Have

With the fishes and loaves, Jesus taught an important spiritual principle: God takes what we have and multiplies it into something far greater.

When Dot and I toured the Holy Land, we were taken to a restaurant by the Sea of Galilee where the most popular dish on the menu is pan fried "Jesus Fish." We ordered one each and found them to be boney but delicious. Everyone was reminded by our tour guide of this miracle story. We marveled that five small fish fed five thousand when we'd just eaten one each.

World Vision may be the most famous charity in the world today feeding hungry people. Millions have been saved from starvation by thousands of donors. Catholic Charities is another worthy example; consistently lauded for keeping overhead costs down and getting every penny possible to those in need. Still another example of fishes and loaves, Salvation Army is literally an army of Christian volunteers, ringing bells for donations and taking food, water, blankets, and medical supplies to victims of fires, floods, tornadoes, and other tragedies. Each of these helpers is the face, hands, and feet of Jesus to someone.

For reflection:
Have you ever been hungry with no prospect for food?
Can you think of other examples where God's law of multiplication is working today?

After a Victory—Watch Out!

After Jesus said his goodbyes and sent the people home, he went up in the hills to pray. His Father had powerfully answered his prayer for provisions. Thousands were fed—body, mind, and spirit. Yet, he sensed this was not a time to celebrate victory but rather to reconnect with his Father.

Here Jesus is teaching us the value of never letting our guard down, to be especially vigilant after a mountaintop victory. This is a dangerous time when Satan seeks to convince us that we're sufficient without God and unplug us from our power-source. Pride can quickly spring up, take root, and lead to disaster.

If Jesus took precautions against cockiness and overconfidence, what of us? Apparently, he also wanted to offer thanksgiving for the day's victory and ask his Father's protection and guidance for tomorrow. Does that sound like a good pattern?

Billy Graham, who died recently, set a sterling example for spiritual leaders everywhere. Early in his ministry, he met with his three principal associates and agreed to establish certain moral guidelines which they all agreed would guide their behavior. Fiduciary honesty and transparency was one. They also agreed that when counseling a member of the opposite sex, they would have a third person present. The result was that this remarkable man was loved and respected by world leaders and commoners alike. They had wisely guarded themselves against scandal and disgrace. We've seen the tragic results of other famous evangelists who failed and destroyed their reputation and God's work by falling to temptation.

For reflection:
Have you experienced temptation after a mountain-top spiritual victory? How will this story help you remain vigilant?

A BIG FISH STORY

(Gospel account in Luke 5:1-11)

Peter and Andrew were fishermen by trade. They'd caught thousands of fish and no doubt loved to swap fish stories with their friends, but this particular fish story topped them all. Here is what happened:

One day as Jesus was preaching on the shore of the Sea of Galilee, great crowds pressed in on him to hear this charismatic street preacher. He noticed two empty boats at the water's edge—their owners had left them and were washing their nets. Stepping into one of the boats, Jesus asked Simon, its owner, to push it out into the water. Then he sat down in the boat and continued teaching the people.

When he finished speaking, he said to Simon, "Now go out where it's deeper and let down your nets, and you will catch many fish."

"But Master, we worked hard all night and didn't catch a thing." You can sense Peter's skepticism that this rabbi is telling him how to fish. "But if you say so, we'll try again."

This time, fish began leaping into their nets. Quickly they filled so full, they began tearing. A shout for help brought their partners in the other boat, and soon both boats were filled with fish and on the verge of sinking.

Background

When he finished speaking, Jesus volunteered to go fishing with Peter and Andrew. Not only that, he gave them an unsolicited fishing tip.

"Go on out where it's deeper and let down your nets, and you'll catch many fish." Peter was caught off guard that Jesus was telling him where to fish. Yet something told Peter to humor Jesus or honor his advice.

"Master, we've fished all night and haven't caught a minnow. But, if you say so, we'll try again." Count Peter and Andrew as skeptics. They had little reason to believe Jesus knew more about fishing than they. James and John were doubters—they didn't even bother to follow when Peter pushed out into deeper water.

Yet, Peter hesitated to refuse Jesus. Maybe he'd seen and heard enough already. Something about this fellow Galilean was pulling Simon like a powerful magnet into his orbit.

Some inner compass caused Peter to waver and give in to Jesus' fishing directions. While he doubted his fishing advice, he didn't doubt Jesus. In fact, he soon turned his back on his fishing vocation to follow him.

Peter and all his companions were awe-struck at the huge pile of fish they had taken. Then Jesus said to Simon Peter, "Don't be afraid; from now on you will be fishing for people!" So, they pulled their boats up on the shore, leaving nets and all, and followed him. Now we see the main point of this big fish story. God had a plan—how about that?

When we throw down our oars and take up his—wondrous things happen. Just ask Peter. The Bible says a wise person is willing to be counseled...

Life Applications

Everyone Has a Fishing License

Dot and I went deep sea fishing on a party boat out of Panama City, FL. Now, I'm supposedly the fisherman of the family but thought it would be fun to take Dot along. You know who caught the biggest fish on the boat that day, don't you? And she's never let me forget it!

Her prize was a 26-pound Red Grouper—so huge she needed a galley mate to help her reel it in. Photos were dutifully taken. When we got back to shore, I was sent to find a cooler and hot ice to preserve Dot's prize fish and take it back home to show off to family.

Back at home, more photos had to be taken. Our youngest daughter Talisa, five or six years old at the time, grudgingly stood beside the monster as Mom held it up to show everyone how humongous it was.

Now, wouldn't it seem that such a fish story needs no embellishment? Yet, each time Dot retells it, her Red Grouper gets bigger and more beautiful—and delicious! Sour grapes? Who, me?

Fishermen sometimes get a bit carried away telling of the big one that got away, how many they caught, and showing with arms outstretched the size of the biggest one. And those fish tales get bigger and better each time they're retold. (Surely, none of you have been so tempted?)

Jesus was fishing for souls. Here we find him surrounded by people, telling them about God.

We too are surrounded by families, neighbors, co-workers, and friends. Random people and strangers cross our paths. We interact with many who don't know the Lord. Jesus wants us to become people persons, sharing the good news of God's unconditional love.

Have you wondered why so many disciples were fishermen? One possible reason was that fishing for a living entails hard work. Rising before daylight, fishermen must round up their bait, nets, and equipment. They must stock their vessel with food and water. By daybreak they are out on the water working hard. When fish are feeding at night—as in this story—they often fished all night, coming home hungry, sleepy, and exhausted.

Jesus was looking for workers, not loafers to join his team. No armchair quarterbacks would do.

Jesus wants to know the same about us.

For reflection:
Do you think the Lord wants you to tell others your faith story?
Will a loved one or co-worker or neighbor be in heaven because you did?

Seizing Opportunities

Jimmy Bennett, whose life story is highlighted elsewhere in this book, has an interesting way of approaching strangers in public places. He watches for anyone who appears to be ill, worried, sick, discouraged, or disoriented—anyone needing a helping hand. He approaches them with a friendly smile, asks if they are okay, and offers to pray for them. "Sure, I may get rejected but that doesn't bother me, I just move on to someone else. You'd be surprised at how many people want to be prayed for—and are open to receiving Christ."

For reflection:
What can we learn from Jimmy's boldness?
Have you ever encountered people needing your help who were also waiting to hear the good news of salvation?

Be Open to the Spirit's Leading

Heather must have been born with a tender heart. When she was old enough to begin babysitting, she chose instead to tutor and help autistic children and those with special needs. Growing up in a family of cat lovers, she stops to pick up and rescue strays left along the roadway. In high school while working during the summer, she found a crippled kitten abandoned in a hospital parking lot and was moved to tears. She brought him home, adopted him, named him P.J., and began nursing him back to health.

At first, P.J. could barely walk, falling and lurching sideways because of what was either an injury or a birth defect. With tender loving care, P.J. became a beautiful and healthy companion.

Understandingly, over the next 15 years P.J. could hardly bear for Heather to leave his side. They became nearly inseparable—all because Heather looked with compassion on one of God's desperate, abandoned, vulnerable, defenseless creations and responded in love. Do you think Jesus was pleased?

For reflection:
Can you recall a time you feel sure you were Spirit-led?
When have you pushed out into the deep when it seemed counter-intuitive?
(How did that turn out?)

A CENTURION'S SERVANT

(Gospel account in Matthew 8:5-13; Luke7:1-10)

When Jesus returned to Capernaum, a centurion's servant was gravely ill and about to die. The Roman military officer had heard of Jesus and sent messengers to him, asking him to come and heal his servant. They came to Jesus and urged him to do it, saying, "If anyone deserves your help, it is he for he loves the Jews and even built a synagogue for us."

So, Jesus went with them. But, before they arrived at the house, the centurion sent friends to say, "Lord, don't trouble yourself coming to my house for I am not worthy of such an honor. I'm even embarrassed to come meet you in person. Just say the word from where you are, and my servant will be healed. I know this because I'm a man under authority of my superiors, with soldiers under me. I tell this one, 'Go!' and he goes and that one, 'Come!' and he comes. I say to my servant, 'Do this!' and he does it.'"

Jesus was impressed by the officer's great faith. Turning to the crowd, he said, "I tell you, I've not seen faith like this in all the land of Israel—even in the very people who're supposed to know all about God."

Then, Jesus said to the officer, "Go home, and what you believe will be done for you." And the officer's servant was healed that very moment.

Background

The Lord had just come down from the mountain where he'd given the most famous of all his teachings—the Sermon on the Mount. "Ask and it will be given to you, seek and you will find, knock and the door will be opened to you." Those following Jesus back down the mountain didn't yet realize they were about to see this spiritual law demonstrated in a real-life crisis.

Please notice that in this miracle Jesus didn't hesitate, equivocate, or interrogate the man but said, "I will go and heal him." Did we miss something here? Wasn't this army officer occupying the Jewish homeland? Wasn't he a "Gentile dog"—a popular term used to describe non-Jews? Wasn't he a pagan man of the world? Instead of subjecting the officer to a board of inquiry, Jesus simply practiced what he preached—when the man asked, Jesus said, "Of course."

Aren't you glad God doesn't ask us to do for others anything he's not willing to do for us? What qualifies one for a miracle? Our highly-educated overly-sophisticated society makes simple things so complicated! Jesus was user-friendly. The Centurion had mastered this lesson: God responds to knocking.

"Lord, I don't deserve to have you in my home!" the centurion protested. This hard-nosed soldier was a man of steel—trained in the art of killing by the Roman military. He knew he was underserving of God's favor. He could not even bring himself to meet Jesus face-to-face.

But whatever he lacked in holiness, he was not without integrity. He didn't harbor an inflated opinion of himself. Yes, he commanded a hundred soldiers, but Jesus commands the armies of heaven. Some inner GPS was pointing him to the One who could save his servant's life.

"Lord, you don't even need to come. If you only say, 'Be healed!' my servant will get well."

What a breath of fresh air from a crusty battle-hardened commander! Not only was he sure Jesus could miraculously heal his servant—he could do it long-distance!

Jesus was so blown away by this Roman commander's faith that he told the crowd, "And I tell you this, many Gentiles will come from all over the world and sit down with Abraham, Isaac, and Jacob at the feast in the Kingdom of Heaven. But many Israelites—those for whom the Kingdom was first prepared—will be cast into outer darkness, where there will be weeping and gnashing of teeth."

The centurion understood, as do all military officers and soldiers, the concept of authority. He knew that Jesus was not acting as a Lone Ranger but a man under his Father's authority, his chain of command.

Jesus himself told us plainly that he does nothing on his own; only what the Father tells him. The centurion got it.

Life Applications

A Crisis Demands Courage

Fritz was a normal-sized baby at birth. "A skinny kid really until I was about 12 years old", Fritz recalls. "My father was a big man, weighing over 300 pounds," Fritz recalls. "I began putting on weight in junior high. By the time I graduated from high school I was about 5' 10" and weighed over 200 pounds."

Fritz enrolled in the University of Pittsburg and joined the Pitt Marching Band. "The next summer I put myself on a diet and lost 50 pounds. When I came back, my band friends didn't recognize me."

Sadly, his success was short-lived. By the time he joined the National Guard and shipped off to boot camp, Fritz tipped the scales at 210 pounds. "Weighing that much makes boot camp a tough place. It took eight weeks of hell to knock off the fat. I came out of there weighing 160 and in the best shape of my life."

After six months of active duty, Fritz was hard as nails. That physique did not last. Outside the strict regime of the military, Fritz lapsed back to super-sizing his meals. He began a high-calorie climb to 310 pounds.

"At Ford Motor Company, a co-worker was also overweight. Our boss got on our case. He became so concerned that he made us weigh in weekly on the company scales and bring him our weight slips. My friend and I began "doctoring" the printouts. We fudged them to show we'd lost a pound or two, but the boss grew suspicious. Finally, he said, 'I'm not buying this. When you get on the scales this time I'm going to see it.' Of course, he caught us red-handed. Still, I wasn't ready to admit it was life threatening until one day when my 300 pound father and I went to a social event. We were standing together when someone came up and asked, 'Are you brothers?' Finally alarm bells went off. I knew things had gone too far." But Fritz did not respond to those alarm bells.

"Another day," he continues, "my friend and I took his kids to the zoo. We parked and had to walk up a small hill to the animal cages. I couldn't do it. Embarrassed, I waited at the car until they returned."

He knew that God was turning up the heat but no one was minding the oven. To get his wife and friends off his case, he made one last half-hearted attempt to lose weight. He cut back on portions and between-meal-snacks and lost 60 pounds, leveling off at around 250 for the next 5 or 6 years.

"I felt better," he says, "and was walking with less difficulty. Still, I avoided exercise and paid no attention to my sugar or fat intake. God's next warning signal came on suddenly: adult on-set diabetes. My blood sugar level skyrocketed. This triggered a blood clot which lodged in my left eye. I was blind in that eye for six months until we found a surgeon who could extract the clotted blood and replace the transparent jelly of the eyeball with synthetic fluid.

His reaction was atypical. "Was I praying all this time?" he comments and answers, "Not really, because I didn't know to. I had no idea that God was interested in my troubles or me. I grew up in a Jewish home, and my family were mostly Jewish by blood. They had no concept of a personal relationship with God. God was patient, though. He was not through with me yet. The diabetes began destroying circulation in my extremities. Gangrene threatened to eat my toes and feet. I was hospitalized for a month as doctors fought to save my foot. What would happen next to get my attention? I can look back now and see that God was not giving up on me. He sent one last messenger, a stroke, leaving me in a half-conscious trance. Time was running out."

"Looking back," Fritz concludes, "it was my dire circumstances that finally brought me to God. My physical body was deteriorating rapidly, and doctors were helpless to reverse the downward spiral. At this black moment a light came on. I knew God was my only hope. Like a drowning man lunging onto a life preserver, I cried out, "Lord, give me another chance at life!" Even though I had not yet given my life to him, God answered that panic-driven prayer. Relief flooded my troubled spirit and I knew that from that day on, I would never be the same. Truly saved by grace. That's my story. I didn't deserve it. I didn't even know how to pray, but when I called out to him, God was there. Now I understand that salvation is not about what we do for God; it's about what Jesus has already done for us. I hope to discover God's plans for the rest of my life. I want to help those in need. I'm still working on that part. Now with God on my side, life is good!"

For reflection:
Have you encountered a problem too big for mortal solutions?
What is the most courageous way to face such crises?

Add to Your Faith Humility

The late Dr. Robert Cook, in his nationally broadcast radio program. "Walk with the King today," told a tender story of taking his 4-year-old daughter out to eat. Playfully, he reached across the table and handed her a menu, knowing she couldn't read. "Honey, what would you like for breakfast?" he asked.

"She inspected the menu carefully, then looked up at me with those adoring blue eyes and whispered, "Daddy, I just want what you want!"

Dr. Cook said, "My heart was flooded with love. I would've given that precious little girl anything in the world that was mine to give."

Dr. Cook then delivered his punch line: "And that's the way it is with our heavenly Father. When we freely yield our will into his, everything he has is ours!"

Oh, the blessings God has in store for hearts of faith and humility!

For reflection:
Does humility come natural to you?
Does the story of this battle-hardened Roman soldier resonate with you?

Understanding Authority

Growing up as a preacher's son, I quickly learned two things about authority: Daddy had it; Momma didn't. Being mischievous and prone to trouble like most preachers' kids, I learned to fear and respect Father because of the painful consequences of folly. Mother, may she rest in peace, was a different story. She was gentle, kind, and loving, and I shamelessly took advantage of her sweet nature. You know the type—when the cat's away, the mice will play! Miraculously, the good Lord has forgiven me.

The Lord invites us to pray in his name. What a far-reaching promise he has given you: Jesus, imbued with omnipotent power from heaven, is inviting you to share in his kingdom power: "Ask for anything in my name, and it will be given to you."

For reflection:
Are you convinced Jesus has been given all his Father's authority?
How does this concept affect your prayers?

A FIG TREE WITHERS AND DIES

(Gospel account in Matthew 21:18-22; Mark 11:12-25)

This is arguably the most difficult of all Jesus' miracles to understand. Obviously, he used it as a teaching opportunity for his disciples. Otherwise it makes no sense.

To be fair, Jesus didn't actually curse the tree as we understand cursing. Certainly, he used no foul language. In our vernacular, we might say he rebuked the tree or condemned it. Pagans might say he put a hex on it. Here's what happened:

The next morning, as Jesus and his disciples were leaving Bethany, Jesus became hungry. He noticed a fig tree beside the road that was in full leaf. He went over to it, expecting to find some ripe figs for breakfast but found nothing except leaves. (It was too early in the season for figs to ripen.)

Disappointed, Jesus said to the tree, "May no one ever eat fruit from you again!" And the disciples heard him say it.

Background

Beginning a hiking trip on an empty stomach is not good. Jesus and his disciples were looking for breakfast as they started out. So, he was delighted to spot a fig tree in full leaf because this usually means ripe figs. What a letdown to find the tree barren! It would be a long hot walk into Jerusalem without food. So, Jesus used the incident as a teaching opportunity.

What can we learn from this strange episode? Let's say God is depending on you, but you're missing in action. Someone needs a kind word or a helping hand but you're unwilling or unavailable. Lost souls are living and dying without Jesus. How tragic when God gives us an opportunity to partner with him but we squander it.

The next day as they were leaving the city, the disciples saw the fig tree shriveled, dead as a doorknob. Peter, remembering what happened the previous day, exclaimed to Jesus, "Look, Teacher, the fig tree you cursed has withered!"

The disciples were amazed. "How did it die so quickly?" they asked. Jesus used their astonishment to teach them the power of believing prayer.

"Have faith in God," Jesus urged them. "I assure you that whoever says to this mountain, 'May God lift you up and throw you into the sea,' and does not doubt in your heart but believes it will happen, it will be done for you."

This dead tree with its withered leaves and drooping limbs was a powerful tutor. "Listen to me!" Jesus told them. "You can pray for anything, and if you believe, you will have it."

Wow! Are you amazed at this promise? So, how do we reach out and take hold of it? Are there no caveats or limits?

His disciples were watching and listening when Jesus rebuked the fig tree. What was that all about? Was our Lord throwing a temper-tantrum? No, he was teaching them about consequences.

Jesus then warned them about one of the deadliest roadblocks to prayer: holding on to hurts, offenses, slights, and wrongs.

"But, when you pray, first forgive anyone you're holding a grudge against, so that your Father in heaven will forgive the wrongs you have done." You know the spiritual law: "Vengeance is mine, I will repay, says the Lord."

Life Applications

When God Calls

A young minister, Dale O'Shields, was on the faculty at Regent University in Virginia Beach when he felt God calling him to move to the Washington, D.C. area to plant a new church. With no family or friends in the area and unsure about where to go, Dale talked with a well-respected senior pastor who pointed him to Gaithersburg, Maryland. He and his wife Terry took a leap of faith, packed their meager belongings and two small children and moved north.

They sold their home in Virginia Beach and cashed in their retirement to rent a temporary residence in Gaithersburg and to get the church started. With Terry and the little girls in tow, he began knocking on doors, meeting neighbors, and inviting those who had no regular place of worship to come and check out their "new church." At the first Sunday morning service, one couple showed up with their five kids. That evening, the family returned.

Church of the Redeemer in the last 32 years has grown into one of the largest in the metropolitan area. Twelve worship services are held each weekend at five campuses, drawing thousands. Services are streamed live online around the world. At Thanksgiving and Christmas, the church works with government social services to provide food and gifts to the needy. Another community outreach is Celebrate Recovery, which helps those struggling with all kinds of addiction. From the start, the church has opened its heart and purse to many world missions.

Again, sensing the Holy Spirit's prompting, Pastor Dale is leading the church to focus on the next generation, offering special activities and worship services to capture the minds and hearts of children and youth. At Easter, special invitations are given to the surrounding community when the congregation presents the Good News of Jesus through a dramatization of the crucifixion and resurrection. This year, more than 30,000 people attended the Easter presentations, and hundreds of those prayed with the pastor to invite Jesus into their lives. Who knows what will happen when God calls and someone answers?

For reflection:
Can you think of a time when you sensed God's call and responded?
How did that turn out?
Has God ever called on you but found you missing in action?

A World of Consequences

Some years ago, our church was asked by a mother to send someone to visit her son in the psychiatric ward of a local hospital. When Dot and I were cleared through locked doors, we found a troubled youth, glad to see us and eager to talk. When we asked him to tell us what was going on, this was his story:

"I'm learning here that my actions have consequences. They give me rules to follow, and if I obey the rules, I can have visitors, make phone calls, and enjoy special privileges. If I refuse to cooperate, they take away my privileges."

We knew his family, so we were amazed that James (not his real name) had grown up in a respectable home with loving parents, yet never been taught something so basic to survival.

Discipline is not in vogue in our progressive, permissive, laissez-faire culture. James was suffering the predictable results, learning in a psych-ward what his father and mother had failed to teach him. Unless we learn to navigate in a world of consequences, we'll travel a bumpy road filled with bruises, pain, and disappointments.

For reflection:
What life experience has best demonstrated
to you the reality of consequences?

Clearing Roadblocks to Prayer Through Forgiveness

When World War II was over, after she was released from the Nazi concentration camp, Corrie ten Boom went back to preach in Germany. Speaking in a German church one day, she was telling the congregation of Jesus' love and mercy. After her message, a man came up to greet her, smiling, "What a fine message, Frau ten Boom. I'm so glad to hear our sins are forgiven."

She recognized him as one of the evil guards who had tortured her and her gentle sister Betsy, forcing them to file past the leering guards, naked and degraded. Betsy died before they were rescued.

"You mentioned you were at Ravensbruck," he continued. "You won't believe this, but I was at Ravensbruck. After the war, I became a Christian. God forgave me. Will you forgive me?"

He extended his weathered, hairy hand. It was as repulsive as a snake. She had a thousand reasons to hate this man. But Betsy would have been first to forgive him. It was perfectly clear in the bible. She looked at the man's repulsive hand. Forgiveness was not an emotion one indulged. It was the will of God. She extended her hand, "I forgive you." (*Corrie ten Boom*, Sam Wellman)

For reflection:
What are you praying for right now?
Are you getting answers to your prayers—or roadblocks?
Does your prayer agree with God's will as you understand it?

A MAN WITH DROPSY

(Gospel account in Luke 14:1-24)

Jesus was invited to eat in the house of a prominent Pharisee. He accepted the invitation though he knew an evil wolfpack was watching him closely, trying to criminalize him. When Jesus arrived, religious big shots kept their eyes peeled, trying to trap him.

There in front of him was a man suffering from edema. Known as dropsy in those days, edema is a painful disease causing one's joints to swell grotesquely. So, Jesus tested the lawyers and Pharisees with a question, "Is it lawful to heal on the Sabbath? Yes or no?"

No one spoke up. So, taking hold of the man, he healed him and sent him on his way.

Background

No cure existed for this dreaded disease called dropsy in those days. It was a death sentence, beyond human help, and excruciatingly painful. Victims also suffered psychologically because the swelling was so disfiguring.

Our world is filled with people coping with "hopeless" problems and prognoses. If you're not squeamish, you might enjoy visiting the National Museum of Health and Medicine just north of the Nation's capital. Prepare to be shocked by the exhibits of people with bizarre and grotesque diseases such as Elephantiasis, a rare form of leprosy, and a human body infested with termites.

You and I may encounter a "hopeless" situation in our future. Or, it may happen to someone we love—family, neighbor, or even a stranger God puts in our path. How will we respond when we come face-to-face with a terminal diagnosis? We believe in God, but do we believe in present-day miracles? Fortunately, this poor bloated man evidently believed Jesus was willing and able to set him free, and so he was a candidate for God's mercy.

This sick stranger was likely not invited to the Pharisee's dinner table, but he crashed the party. This took courage born of desperation. If the prominent host had spotted him before he got to Jesus, he may have thrown him out in the street.

You may come up against man-made rules or social protocols blocking you from getting life-saving help. And if one's life is at stake, rules can't be allowed to stand in the way.

Are you surprised that Jesus was invited to dinner by a highly-placed Pharisee? Or, that he accepted the man's hospitality—knowing he was walking into a trap? Yes, it seemed out-of-character for the religious bigwigs to want to eat and hobnob with Jesus after all the times he denounced them. And that Jesus would accept such an invitation makes little sense on the surface.

Yet, look at what happened. A man was suffering. Jesus did not hesitate, risking arrest to heal him as the self-important religious hot dogs sat gawking, grousing, and grumbling!

Jesus sensed in his heart he should say yes to this odd dinner invitation. He was being lead and guided by the Holy Spirit.

Jesus knew the Pharisees were lying in the weeds for him, a Southern colloquium for predators hiding to pounce on their prey. They would use any excuse to do their dirty work—in this case preparing a banquet and inviting him as guest of honor. Jesus read their evil minds and black hearts. He could have healed the man privately—without upsetting his host. Instead, with all the guests at this lavish dinner party watching, he confronted them: "If one of you has a son or ox that falls into a well on the Sabbath day, wouldn't you rush to pull him out?"

Trapped in their own conniving snare, his enemies fell silent.

Hopefully, such a life-threatening confrontation is not in your future. If that moment comes, however, you've been schooled by the Lord. The Holy Spirit will show you what to do when the time comes.

My wife has a gentle way of keeping me grounded. "You'll never regret doing the right thing!" she likes to say. "Put things back in the place you found them." she reminds me. "Don't put off until tomorrow what needs doing today." Some folks need a lot of supervision!

Life Applications

When All Seems Hopeless

Alice Faye Brown's story is living proof that with God no situation is hopeless. Her story is one of hopeless turned to hope. In her words:

"I was born into a family so deeply damaged and addicted to alcohol, they were totally unable to care for me. Separated from my siblings when I was three years old, my life became a straitjacket of strict religious rules. Yet, those legalistic rules did not keep me from being traumatized at the age of eight when three men, two family members and a minister, sexually abused me. I learned very quickly to keep secrets and deceive people. At eight or nine, I found a way to secretly get into alcohol which became my outlet.

At sixteen, I was allowed to marry only to find I had been sold to my husband in exchange for a monthly payment of money! After this latest betrayal, I walked away from God and became a closet alcoholic. Abused by my husband, I spent time in the hospital, coming home to find he'd set fire to the house where my two young children and I were living. He was sentenced to five years in prison for arson.

Filing for divorce, I returned to the loving arms of Jesus who graciously took me in.

I met and married my second husband in church, at age 21. We played guitar and accordion and sang gospel songs on stage for many years. Incredibly, after three more children and many years of marriage, I lost my way again, returning to the gutter of alcohol, and was again divorced.

My broken life became one of total drunkenness, immorality, and doing time in three rehabilitation centers—none of which worked for me. Through all of it, Jesus never gave up on me. He always sent someone to remind me that He was still there. Finally, I again surrendered and returned to God who gave me a place in my new church, serving in Cancer Care ministry.

Eighteen years ago, I was diagnosed for the second time with a rare type of cancer called GIST. Told my cancer was inoperable and incurable, I spent the next ten years in chemotherapy which finally stopped working. The tumors were so aggressive I was accepted into a painful 2-year trial at the National Institutes of Health where I was given daily oral chemo and bi-weekly infusions. Then abruptly those treatments also stopped working, leaving me no choice but surgery to try and save my life. Through it all, Jesus never left me. Without him, I would not have come through those two major surgeries alive. A drastic measure was taken, and a permanent colostomy became my new way of life. After three more surgeries, I'm cancer free and have been for five wonderful years—all praise to God! Now, I wouldn't trade my life for anything because the Lord is using my past to help me empathize, pray for, counsel, and tell others, 'Don't ever give up on yourself, because God will never give up on you.'"

For reflection:
Have you ever asked God for an extra spoonful of faith to cope with your impossibilities?

Let the Spirit Lead

A lady described to her New Believers class how her life had been falling apart. Her husband had lost his job and was drinking heavily. They couldn't pay their bills, and their children suffered from the high tensions from a marriage breaking apart. None of them were Christians, but the lady knew something was missing in their lives.

One Sunday morning, the woman felt a compelling need to get out of the house. She got up early, made a cup of coffee, took her keys, got in her car, and started driving aimlessly around town. On a quiet street in Old Town Gaithersburg, she noticed a sign on an industrial-looking building: "Church of the Redeemer."

'That's strange!' she thought. She had never seen that sign before. Feeling a sudden urge to check it out, she parked the car and ventured inside, not knowing if the public was welcome.

A worship service had just started. An usher welcomed her inside, She took a seat in the back row. The music and message were like nothing she'd ever heard. When the pastor gave an altar call, she felt herself being drawn to the front. Now, she knew the Holy Spirit had been leading her.

She gave her life to the Lord that day. She and her husband are still struggling, but instead of anger and fear, she has a deep inner peace. She knows God will see her through.

For reflection:
Have you ever found that life is less complicated than you have made it—once you allow the Holy Spirit to lead you? What was the story? How did you learn this?

Watch Your Motives

The Chairman of the Nuclear Regulatory Commission once sent me to work with a U.S. Congressman who was writing legislation to govern the disposal of high-level radioactive waste. Soon after I reported for duty, a reporter asked me to describe the legislation being crafted. Unfortunately, I was prominently quoted in his story.

The Congressman's staff director called me in for a Dutch uncle counseling session. "We don't have a lot of rules around here but there's one you don't want to break: Don't get your name in the paper or on TV." He went on to explain, "The Congressman is the one elected by the voters, and he runs for re-election every two years. So, all credit, all attention, all publicity must go to him and him alone. It's really very simple, there's only one show horse in this rodeo—all the rest of us are work horses."

His message was clear: You must always seek to make the boss look good. This means turning all favorable light on him. After the staff director's timely advice, I was careful to watch my motives.

For reflection:
Knowing God is watching our motives, will you monitor yours?
Which of your motives are self-serving?
Where are you becoming more like Jesus?

JARIUS' DAUGHTER RAISED

(Gospel account in Matthew 9:18-26; Mark 5:21-43; Luke 8:40-56)

When Jesus came back across the Sea of Galilee, a crowd gathered. A synagogue ruler named Jarius came and fell at his feet, pleading with him to heal his little daughter. "She's about to die!" he cried in desperation. "Come and put your hands on her so she can get well and live."

When they arrived at Jairus' house, Jesus would not let anyone go in with him except Peter, James, John, and the child's father and mother. Meanwhile, people inside the house were already holding a wake for the girl, wailing and mourning.

Jesus confronted them, "Why all this weeping and commotion? The child isn't dead; she is only sleeping." Oh, how the crowd scoffed at this, laughing in his face. He quietly told them all to go outside. Jesus had faced scorners and unbelievers before. He didn't waste time arguing with them but simply ushered them out of the house.

The crowd knew the girl was dead because their eyes told them so. Jesus knew what he was going to do. He was not overwrought by their hooting and hollering. He was not going to be distracted. Don't miss this spiritual insight: When you face scoffers, ignore them; just do whatever God has put in your heart.

After sending the unbelieving crowd outside, Jesus took the child's parents and the disciples and went into the room where the girl was lying. Taking her by the hand, he said to her, "Little girl, I say to you, get up!" And the child, who was 12 years old, stood up and walked around! Luke put it this way: "Her spirit returned and she jumped out of bed and walked around!"

Her parents were astonished—absolutely overwhelmed. Jesus ordered them not to tell anyone what happened. Then, he asked them to get her something to eat. Jesus' tender words to the little girl were loaded with power. As John wrote, "For as the Father raises the dead and gives them life, so also the Son gives life to whom he will." (John 5:21)

The child's parents were unable to keep a secret! Who could blame them? Their news spread like a polar vortex howling down from the North Pole! Jesus was trying to work quietly, out of reach of those wanting to kill him before he finished his redemptive mission, but people were spilling the beans, telling of this miracle-worker in the towns, over the countryside, in the valleys, and on the mountains! People in darkness, fearing death and the grave, were seeing a great light. The true light had come into the world; their long night was over.

Background

Oh, how Jesus cherished little ones! Of all the things to admire about our Lord, his love for children was heart-warming. He enjoyed gathering them up in his arms and blessing them. And, how they loved him! His apostles kept trying to shoo the kids away, fearing they were distracting the Messiah from more important things.

"Let the children come to me. Don't stop them, for the kingdom of God belongs to such as these." Jesus was rebuking them for their misguided loyalty. One can almost hear him saying, "More important things? There are no more important things!"

Jesus went with Jarius, no questions asked. As far as we know, our Lord never turned away a single person who came to him in need. Jewish leaders were divided in their opinions of Jesus. Some welcomed him, but most were fearful or jealous. To save his daughter, this highly respected Jewish ruler swallowed his pride and strangled his prejudices. Our independent-minded society boasts, "If it is to be, it's up to me." With his young daughter's life at stake, Jairus couldn't afford such swelling pride. A noble act of humility was required for Jairus to come pleading, especially to a controversial young rabbi. But, what wonderful possibilities were birthed when he fell at Jesus feet and worshipped him!

As Jarius led Jesus toward his dying daughter's sickbed, messengers arrived with bad news. "Your daughter is dead. Don't trouble the teacher anymore."

Can you believeyy such an aloof attitude? No sympathy—just deal with it and move on! Go on home and bury the girl and stop bothering Jesus!

These same friends were likely unhappy with Jairus for appealing to Jesus. You can almost hear them harping, "Just imagine our esteemed leader groveling to this Johnny-come-lately!"

Have you ever been the victim of thoughtless advice?

"Just turn it over to the Lord!" when you're grieving the loss of a loved one.

"Just say all is well!' another may insist—when all is certainly not well.

Jarius' friends no doubt meant well. (So did Job's friends.) But well-meaning friends can unintentionally do more damage than good. Better had they prayed and kept silent.

What is a Christ-like attitude toward misguided givers of bad advice? Assuming they mean well is a good place to start—that they're motivated by love. People may be hurting for you but don't know what to say. Like Peter, they often say it anyway. Whatever comes to mind, they spout it out without filter. Maybe you've been guilty, too?

Jesus overheard the tragic news messengers brought. Ignoring their comments, he told the synagogue ruler, "Don't be afraid; just believe, and your daughter will be healed." So, they kept on walking and talking. Can you imagine the furious battle of faith and doubt, struggling to take control of this grieving father? Somehow, Jarius ignored his well-meaning friends and entrusted himself to Jesus. What a revealing moment for us! Your faith may also be tested by fire. Will you give in to your doubts and give up on God?

Life Applications

Overcoming our Hubris

If we don't get it, God has a way of keeping us humble. On a visit to Jerusalem, our tour guide took us to the Western Wall (formerly called the Wailing Wall), one of the most sacred places in the Holy City. Men and women were separated; my friend John and I were given a skull cap and invited to quietly approach the wall, lay our hands on it and pray. I was so excited, telling John, "I really feel like God is going to speak to me today!"

We tip-toed up to the wall, lifted our hands to touch it and began praying. Suddenly, I felt a strangely warm/wet sensation hit the back of my neck and travel down my back. When John finished praying I turned around to ask him what had happened. "Well, I think God may have sent you the message you were looking for!" One of Jerusalem's countless pigeons had relieved itself on my head. O Lord, you have a balloon-bursting sense of humor—and I get the point!

For reflection:
What circumstances have humbled you?
What would you like Jesus to do for you or yours?

His Welcome Mat is Out

When this rabbi came and fell at Jesus' feet, he had no way of knowing what kind of response to expect. Jesus had certainly not been treated well by his own religious authorities. Yet, this was a fellow human being in deep agony, and the Lord immediately welcomed him. What does Jarius' miracle say to us? The Lord will welcome you! "He who comes to me I will in no way cast out." Try to remember Jairus' wonderful story when you face a defining moment, when your life hangs by a thread—or someone needs a miracle.

Kari Engen can tell you a lot about kids in need of miracles. Kari was a young teenager growing up in affluent Rockville, Maryland when she rode an old school bus to Mexico on a mission trip with her local church. The poor orphans and homeless street kids stole her heart. Kari sensed God calling her to help them. When the door closed on that Mexico mission work, Kari went up on a rooftop one day to ask God, "What now, Lord?" She sensed God calling her to Guatemala.

With the help of friends, she went to Guatemala City and set up a ministry for street kids. One day, a local pastor took her to the city's main garbage dump where whole families live in makeshift tents, eating only what they can scavenge off the dump. The children had no schools or health care. Kari moved to the dump and lived there for a year, winning the trust of both parents and children. The next year, she rented a building next to the dump and opened a school. About 35 homeless kids showed up. That was in 1988.

Today, Mi Refugio mission has a teaching staff of 19 Guatemalan teachers helping Kari with classes from preschool through high school. "Every day, our mission is to bring Jesus' unconditional love and presence to our 400 students at our 12-acre San Pedro campus. From preschool through high school; from career school to the university; 38 teachers, administrators, cooks, bus drivers, maintenance people, and I abide by this mission." Kari says.

Medical clinics are given free each year to about 2000 impoverished souls. Each school child is given a healthy breakfast, lunch, snacks, and vitamins. Bags of food are sent home to kids with single moms.

Many of Kari's former students are following what God has planted in their hearts, studying to become physicians, computer scientists, psychologists, administrators, lawyers, and judges to name a few.

"Who can be compared with God enthroned on high? He stoops to look, and lifts the poor from the dirt, and the hungry from the garbage dump, and sets them among princes." (Ps. 113:5-7 TLB)

Kari will tell you our Lord loves every one of those little children. That's why He sent her to help them.

For reflection:
His arms are open wide, his mercy yours for the asking.
How have you asked?
He has sent us on a hugging mission to a hurting world;
where do you fit in?

Persevering Trust

Peggy's colon cancer spread to her liver. Stage four, inoperable, terminal. Would she fall away or keep trusting God?

"I've rested my case with the Lord," she told us.

How can that be? Only by God's grace could she stubbornly persevere and keep on trusting in the face of tragic news. Peggy decided to throw her lot in with God, holding onto his dear hand while passing through her darkest valley. Her testimony was marvelous: "I am at perfect peace!"

A songwriter called it, "Peace like a river in my soul." Peggy's victory was already won. All that remained was her homecoming celebration!

For reflection:
Where have you persevered, trusting in God,
when all evidence was screaming, "Give up?"

A LEPER IN GALILEE

(Gospel account in Matthew 8:1-4; Mark 1:40-45; Luke 5:12-16)

After healing Peter's mother-in-law and many other sick people who came to him that night, Jesus rose up early the next morning. While it was still dark, he left Peter's house and went off to a solitary place to pray.

A man suffering from leprosy came to him, knelt down, and begged for help.

"If you want to," he said, "you can make me clean."

Jesus, filled with compassion, reached out and touched him.

"I do want to," he answered. "Be clean!" At once, the disease left the man.

Background

The night before had been one of those mountain-top experiences. That evening after sunset people brought to Jesus many suffering various kinds of diseases, and laying his hands on each one, he healed them. Demons came out of people, shouting, "You are the Son of God!"

So, why would an exhausted Jesus force himself out of bed while his disciples were still sleeping and slip out to a lonely place to pray? He was staying grounded, going back to his Father for communion. He knew Satan was looking for opportunities to discredit and destroy his ministry. Losing yesterday's battle, his adversary would be even more determined to defeat him today.

Our Lord let neither sleep nor exhaustion keep him from this vital appointment. He was committed to daily life-altering time with his Father—talking with him about yesterday's victories and today's opportunities. He needed today's marching orders. And, he simply loved those precious moments alone with his Abba.

When the disciples awoke and found Jesus gone, they quickly formed a search party and went looking for him. Knowing he treasured his private time alone with God, they went out into the wilderness. Sure enough, they soon found him.

Meanwhile, word had leaked out that Jesus was missing so the locals joined the search party. When they found him, they tried to keep him from leaving their community. But he told them, "I must preach the good news of the Kingdom of God to the other towns also, because that is why I was sent."

Would Jesus have blessed that town by staying longer? No doubt, he could have healed more people and won more hearts to God. So why did he insist on leaving? He was being led by the Holy Spirit. In those pre-dawn communion times, his Father must have told him it was time to move on. So, he left there and kept on preaching in the synagogues of Judea. He stayed intimately connected with the Father—and those crucial times of communion kept him focused. Grounded and guided. Plugged into the power source.

Taking Time to Pray

When I've hurt someone's feelings or missed a golden opportunity to help them, it's often because I've failed to slow down long enough to pray. Oh, the miraculous difference between walking with God and traveling alone!

For my friend, Betty, her daily prayer time—and grounding—is a noon prayer service at a church near her office. That God also values her being present at the prayer service became absolutely clear to her one day when she had a meeting in another town a short distance away from her office and the church. The meeting ended with just enough time for her to swing through the McDonald's drive-through and pick up something for after the prayers. Perfect timing—or so it seemed.

As she approached the McDonald's parking lot, she had to drive past a beggar, holding a sign, saying that he was hungry. Now, her practice with hungry beggars is to invite them in for a meal and spend some time with them, getting to know them. In this case, she had no cash in the car, had she wanted to hand over a few dollars. Feeling guilty but using the excuse that she did not have time to stop without missing Mass, she drove past the hungry beggar and ordered her food. When she came around the side of the parking lot to leave, the entrance and exit being the same road, she once again saw the beggar.

"Oh, well," she thought. "Feed the hungry as God has directed us to do (in the words of Jesus, 'what you do for the least of them you do for me') or take care of my spiritual needs?" Feed the hungry, she decided, assuming that in this case God would take care of her spiritual needs.

So, she pulled over to the beggar and asked if he would meet her inside. He agreed. She parked and got in line with him, having time to talk to him about what had put him out on the street while they were waiting to place their order.

It did not take long for the whole process to be finished, but it was just long enough that she knew she would miss the prayer service. Nonetheless, she drove to the church. Maybe it would run longer; maybe she would be able to catch the last few minutes or spend some after-service time with the pastor.

As she drove up, she recognized parishioners' cars parked outside. Still there! As she entered the church, she discovered that the prayer service had not yet begun. The pastor had been delayed; everyone had been informed and had waited. So, Betty actually arrived on time. It was as if God had stopped the clock for her! The most obvious explanation for her is that God, too, wanted her to have time for prayer—because he considers it important, as Jesus demonstrated.

For reflection:
Have you noticed the difference prayer makes in your working day? What happens on those days you take time to be with God—spending time with him, listening for his voice? How does that compare with those days when time presses in and you rush out without refreshing your spirit.

The Lord is Willing

The leper, no doubt, had good reason to wonder if he was a candidate for God's mercy. Don't you have those moments? Am I worthy? No. Do I deserve good things from God? No. Have I sinned and broken God's laws? Yes.

Bruce came home from World War II where he'd been twice wounded and suffering from the aftermath of a shell exploding next to him. (Post-traumatic stress syndrome was not in the medical jargon at the time.) He was having problems holding on to his faith. "My life is such a mess, I just don't think God wants to get involved!" His father, who was also a minister, kept praying for his wounded son and counseling him. Finally, his hovering dark clouds lifted and Bruce understood that the Lord indeed feels our pains and heals our wounds.

For reflection:
Have you ever suffered from low self-esteem?
What would it do for you to hear the Lord say, "Of course, I'm willing!"?

Staying Grounded and Guided

When we allow ourselves to become separated from God, bad things happen. We begin to flounder, straining vainly to solve impossible issues—in other words, become our own god. When we find ourselves trying to solve the world's problems or even extricate ourselves from the cauldron, it's often because we failed to slow down long enough to share our concerns and troubled emotions with God. Oh, the miraculous difference between walking with God and traveling alone!

"I was living in constant fear of rejection," recalls Robyn Kam, "working hard to please everyone, including the Lord. Then, I came to realize I am valuable in Jesus' eyes and I don't have to work to earn his love. I have found security in Christ and don't live in fear of rejection anymore. I no longer try to please everyone, changing my personality to please those around me. I have learned to be me, a daughter loved by Christ and now I can love others with the love the Lord has given me." (Used by permission.)

Whether we are afraid of rejection or quite confident in ourselves and our faith, we all need to stay grounded and guided and will experience some challenges in doing so. A time came in my career when nothing seemed to be going right. A new President of the United States had been elected, quickly sweeping out the door all the past President's senior managers, replacing them with "his team." A retired General was appointed to head up safety and safeguards at the Nuclear Regulatory Commission. He came in with the attitude that everything done before his arrival was a disaster, the staff was inept, and he was the only one who could set things straight. (Is this sounding vaguely familiar? Maybe you've been in this same boat?) Nothing we could do pleased him. If he'd been given the power, I think he would've abolished the whole agency and started from scratch. The professional staff began looking for exit doors, reassignments, transfers, or early retirements. I found the only way to remain sane until the tempest was past was by cleaving closer to God. Eventually, it was the General who found greener pastures. Next day, the hailstorm stopped, the sun came out, and untold prayers were answered!

For reflection:
How does God guide you?
In what ways does prayer make your work more fruitful?

A TOUR OF GALILEE

(Gospel account in Matthew 4:23-25; Mark 1:35-39; Luke 4: 42-44)

Jesus then went throughout Galilee, teaching in their synagogues, telling God's good news of salvation to all who would listen, and healing every kind of sickness. News of the man from Galilee spread all over Syria. People brought to him all who were ill of various diseases, those suffering severe pain, the demon-possessed, those having seizures, and the paralyzed, and he healed them.

Large crowds began following him, eager to be a part of this special moment in history. Everywhere he went, he taught people the truth—that beginning today you can experience a new life in God's kingdom. Word got around that a new kind of teacher had arrived—one who was confirming his gospel message with miraculous healings.

Background

After Peter's mother-in-law and many others were healed, you may recall Jesus disappeared to be alone with God and pray. The disciples formed a search party and went looking for him. "Everyone is looking for you!" they told him. You can sense them urging Jesus to get back quickly while the crowds were still hungering to hear more. But Jesus wasn't marching to their drums.

So, Jesus led the disciples through Galilee on a wonderfully fruitful mission trip. The disciples were soaking it all in, being trained for the soon-coming day when the mantle of Christ would fall on them. God's wandering flocks were being gathered up in the Shepherd's arms and gently carried back into the Kingdom by his anointed preaching, teaching, and healing miracles. And the Holy Spirit was guiding, anointing, and confirming everything he did.

"You will do even greater things than these," Jesus told his marveling companions, "but wait until the Holy Spirit comes upon you." Sure enough, they huddled in a secret room after his death and resurrection—waiting to receive the Lord's promise. When the day of Pentecost finally arrived, they were anointed with astonishing powers to continue Christ's redeeming ministry.

This tour of Galilee was also boot camp for the disciples. Jesus was showing them how to honor God by loving his people—not just healing their bodies but also forgiving their sins, listening to their complaints, empathizing with them, absorbing their loneliness, sensing their despair, and feeling their pains.

The apostle Paul later painted a portrait of Jesus' lifestyle in 1 Corinthians 13: "Love is patient and kind, keeps no record of wrongs. Love never gives up." Jesus taught that all who sin become sin's slaves. You've seen it, people caught up in generational curses and wholly powerless to free themselves. Thanks be to God, Jesus didn't leave us hopeless but gave us the key to unlock our shackles.

"You will know the truth, and the truth will set you free," he promised. In this tour of Galilee, Jesus was painting this promise on the canvass of life in living color. He was telling people the truth—and they were being liberated, emancipated, redeemed, and restored.

Israel was all about religion. And religion had suffered a spiritual collapse, falling into a system of do's and don'ts. The religious gatekeepers had concocted a rigid code of rules to please God and prove themselves worthy. Then came Jesus, bringing the good news that God loves us, period. We don't have to earn his love by proving to him we're perfect. Does this new way appeal to you?

When the Lord came to Israel, bringing unconditional love, that love itself may have spoken louder than his sermons. Sometimes all love has to do is to show up.

Life Applications

A Sense of Destiny

No," Jesus told those surrounding him when they urged him to stay, "it's time to move on to other places so I can preach to them also. That is why I have come." His radar was pointed directly toward the Father's will, a Holy Spirit imparted sense of destiny.

Cleft palate is a deformity causing shame and suffering to millions of children. This disfiguring condition usually causes a speech defect as well. The good news is that trained surgeons in most cases can join the two split parts of the palate back together. The speaking and cosmetic effects are amazing: what some might consider a pitiful creature transformed into a perfectly normal-looking-and-sounding kid. Sadly, thousands of these children are isolated in third world countries with no doctors or hospitals to perform this life-altering surgery. Enter Smile Train and other Christian mission groups that volunteer to rescue these unfortunate victims, often flying them to the United States free of charge. Why would surgeons give up tens of thousands of dollars to perform such services free? The answer is obvious: they do it out of a God-given sense of destiny. What a noble response to take one's God-given skills and use them to set free penniless young children who would otherwise go through life damaged and demeaned.

For reflection:
What do you sense is your God-given destiny?
What is most likely to distract you?

Futility or Fruitfulness?

Robert was a blond suntanned surfer living the hippy life on the beaches of California. "I had no other ambitions," he said. He was thinking, 'This life is as good as it gets. Every day, from sunrise to sunset, riding those wonderful waves—what could possibly be greater than this?"

Then, an older lady took an interest in their little surfing cult. "She began bringing sandwiches to the beach and talking to us about this guy Jesus," Robert shared.

Something clicked in Robert's heart from these discussions, and he gave his life to the Lord. People told him not to bother going to college, he would never make it. He ignored their advice, went to Bible College, married his sweetheart Karen, and together moved to Peru to found Camino de Vida, a nationwide Christian ministry.

Today Robert pastors one of the largest churches in Peru. He has established orphanages, schools, medical missions, and Pastors' conferences, touching thousands of lives.

For reflection:
How can you become a fishing companion of Jesus?
What opportunities do you see beckoning?

The Theology of Just Showing Up

Years ago, a man in our church lost his wife to alcoholism. What words can alleviate such a tragic loss? One day, soon after the funeral, I happened to be walking by his computer store when the Spirit spoke silently: "Stop what you're doing, go into his store, and speak to John." I had no clue how to comfort him so I walked on past. Again came a strong impression, "Go back and try." I turned around and entered his store.

When John saw me, his whole face lit up; he rushed down the aisle to give me a bear hug. I still had no idea what to say but fumbled my way through, telling him how we loved his wife and how saddened we were at his loss.

After a few painfully awkward moments, I bid John goodbye and left, feeling I had failed miserably. However, for a long time afterward, every time I saw John, he would tell me how much it meant when I dropped by. And, all I did was show up.

For reflection:
That love never gives up—how has this truth impacted your life?
When have you experienced the joy of just "being there"
for someone in a crisis?

JESUS PAYS HIS TAXES

(Gospel account in Matthew 17:24-27)

The tax man cometh—even for Jesus! After the Lord and his disciples arrived in Capernaum, tax collectors from the temple came to Peter and asked him, "Doesn't your teacher pay his taxes?"

"Of course, he does," Peter assured them. Then, he went into the house to tell Jesus about it, but Jesus already knew.

Before Peter had a chance to speak, Jesus asked: "Simon, what do you think? When a king levies taxes, who pays? Does the king tax his own people or the foreigners he has conquered?

"He taxes the foreigners," Peter replied.

"Then his citizens get off free, right? But we don't want to offend them. So, go down to the lake, and throw in a line. Open the mouth of the first fish you catch, and you'll find a coin. That coin will be sufficient for both of us. Take it and pay our taxes."

Background

Jesus told Peter to do a very strange thing: "Go down to the lake and cast in a line. Open the mouth of the first fish you catch and you will find a coin. Take it and go pay our taxes."

Peter's mouth must have flown open like the fish! Can you imagine how many flouncing fish this weather-beaten angler had dragged out of that lake? And, how many of them had swallowed coins? So, how would Peter respond to his teacher's crazy, way-out suggestion? Over the years, he'd hauled in thousands of fish. To the best of his memory, every one of them was flat broke, not even a widow's mite! If Peter hadn't trusted Jesus, he would've laughed in his face, but he'd seen too much to doubt him now. There was much he still didn't understand about his beloved rabbi—but he'd never misled Peter or the disciples. Everything he told them had proven true. So, Peter took a deep breath, threw logic to the wind, and went fishing! He was learning to trust Jesus even when logic was screaming, "This is insane!"

So, you marvel at this unique miracle but think, "Well, that was Jesus teaching Peter to trust him. He would never do anything that far out for me, right?" Don't be so sure.

Haven't you heard of God stepping into someone's world to bring a life-saving miracle or to meet a pressing need? Maybe you've come up against giants and wondered if you would survive—yet God rescued you. As the song says so beautifully, "God will make a way when there seems to be no way!" Maybe your taxes didn't get paid like Peter's. Maybe your miracle was a check that showed up unexpectedly, a friend who dropped by when you were lonely and desperate, a malignant X-ray that turned out to be a false positive, or a failing marriage or relationship that ended up restored. When you needed him most, God came through.

How did our Lord walk that tightrope—between worldly and divine? The miracles give us some important clues. He was respectful of authority. He kept the laws of the land. He loved family and enjoyed his friends. He lived to do God's will. He did it God's way—and would not be diverted by fear nor influenced by popular opinion.

Jesus knew this tax story would get back to his enemies. The Pharisees and Sadducees would not be deterred, they would still find a way to destroy him. They would join an unholy alliance with Rome to kill him—and they would have their pound of flesh. Of this, Jesus had no doubts.

But their evil designs could not stop him from doing what he came to earth to accomplish. Saving his skin was never high on his priority list—in fact, it didn't even register! He knew what lay ahead. Setting his eyes toward Jerusalem, toward the cross, he ignored his enemies and kept on doing his Father's work.

Our Lord was on a mission from heaven, helping earthlings find their way back to God. His was the ultimate purpose-driven life. He came down from heaven to bring us up to heaven, to open the door, to tell us the Father is waiting for us—that God has left his porch light burning. Through his presence on earth, he modeled the ways in which God wants us to obey. What would Jesus do? Is always a good question to ask when in doubt.

Life Applications

Rendering Unto Ceasar

Some Christian sects have decided they're responsible to no one but God. Not surprisingly, the IRS takes a dim view of such theology. Jesus agreed with the tax collectors. He acknowledged we're citizens of heaven, yes, but also citizens of earth. As citizens, our duty is to obey the government that protects us from anarchy.

A couple found their IRS tax obligation difficult to meet. They had just returned from working in Jordan in August and, upon turning in their tax paperwork that they had been given permission to delay until October, were surprised by a tax bill of $11,000. Their return had used up all their resources; their bank account was close to zero. They asked the IRS for an extension to pay, and they were given six weeks, a firm deadline. They were employed, but their ordinary salaries would not cough up that kind of additional cash. They had no friends or relatives who could lend them that much, either. So, they did the only thing they could. They turned the problem over to God. The following week, the wife received a check for $3000 from a university where she had worked ten years prior, stating that since no additional deposits had been made in a decade, the university had to return the monies she had paid into a retirement fund. She was young enough to make up that amount of money before retiring, so she and her husband rejoiced at the good luck and would have marveled at the coincidence but they had come to rely on God for those kinds of miracles. Realizing that they had not only been handed some money but also a path toward a solution, the wife contacted the other university at which she had worked, paid into the pension fund, and then left. Sure enough, there was $2,000 available through that fund, and the university was willing to pay it out immediately. Then she checked her 403B fund from another previous job. Yes, it could be paid out, too, and there was $3,500 in that fund. The request to withdraw and close the account was taken over the phone; she was assured that the request would be processed in the morning and whatever the balance was at that time would be sent to her immediately. They were quite close: $8,500 between the three checks. That exhausted all retirement funds, and they had no savings because they had used all their savings to return to the USA. They were not worried, however. They assumed that God would take care of the remaining $2,500. They were mostly curious as to where it would come from. Two days before the taxes had to be mailed in, the final check, from the 403B fund, showed up: $6,000.

Certain that there was some kind of mistake and hesitant to cash an incorrect check, the wife called the 403B fund manager. He confirmed that the amount was correct. He had placed much of her account in Apple stock, and the iPhone had come out that day, creating a big spike for all who had funds in Apple. The amount was correct as of the morning the check was issued—and the couple was able to pay their taxes in full. Sort of like a coin in a fish's mouth!

For reflection:
When has God showed up in your life in a surprising way?

Guard Your Attitude

Did you hear about the young boy who wanted a hundred dollars? He prayed for two weeks but got no response? Discouraged, he sat down and wrote God a letter: "Dear Mr. God, I really need a hundred dollars. Yours truly, Billy."

When a postal worker saw the envelope addressed to God, she didn't know what to do with it so she sent it to the White House. The President smiled and told his secretary, "Send the little guy five bucks. That should look like a large sum of money to one so young."

The boy was delighted and sat down to write God a thank you note. "Dear Mr. God, thanks for sending me the hundred bucks. However, I notice that you sent it through Washington, D.C., and as usual, the government deducted ninety-five percent!"

Jesus told Peter, "Let's not disrespect the tax collectors. They're only doing their job." Jesus was teaching us that government may not be popular—but it's necessary to hold together the fabric of society. As loyal citizens, we must guard our attitude—trying to see the good instead of magnifying the bad.

For reflection:
What's your attitude toward paying taxes? About tithing?
(Our pastor says, God loves a cheerful giver
but he'll accept it from a grouch!)

Partners With God

In the spring of 2017, Pope Francis shocked the world by begging forgiveness for the "sins and failings of the church and its members" during the 1994 Rwanda genocide. In a meeting with Rwandan President Paul

Kagame, he acknowledged that the church itself bore blame, as well as some priests and nuns who "succumbed to hatred and violence, betraying their own evangelical mission" by participating in the killings when more than 80,000 of their fellow citizens were slaughtered. Many died at the hands of priests, clergymen, and nuns, according to accounts by survivors, and the Rwandan government says many died in the churches where they had sought refuge. In that historic meeting, Pope Francis expressed the desire that "this humble recognition of the failings of that period...may promote hope, renewed trust, and a future of peace." (Associated Press, 3/21/17)

Today we are seeing a land changing its long-held attitudes regarding women—to protect their role in the workplace, root out sexual harassment, and expose exploitation including both blatant and subtle discrimination. Long overdue, society is finally grappling with problems of racial attitudes, including racial profiling, equality in salaries and promotions, interracial marriages, and other forms of prejudice.

Christians who fail to treat our fellowman with dignity and respect have no excuse. Jesus has shown us the way.

For reflection:
What are you modeling for those watching your life?
Where do others see Jesus in you?

JESUS WALKS ON WATER

(Gospel account in Matthew 14:22-33; Mark 6:45-52)

After Jesus fed the multitude, he told his disciples to get back in the boat and return to the other side of the lake while he dismissed the crowd. After saying his goodbyes, he climbed up a mountain to pray.

Soon, a strong storm blew in upon the Sea of Galilee. The disciples were far out from shore when the fierce squall began battering their small boat. Suddenly a human form appeared in the driving wind, walking on the water.

"It's a ghost!" they cried out in panic as the figure approached, stepping on the high waves. They were terrified, but Jesus spoke soothingly to them, "Take courage; it's me. Don't be afraid."

"Master if it's really you, bid me come to you on the water," Peter, suddenly bold, called out.

"Come on over!" yelled Jesus, possibly with a smile on his face.

Clambering out of the boat, Peter started to walk on the water toward Jesus, but when he looked down at the raging waves, he lost his new-found courage. Beginning to sink, he screamed, "Lord, save me!"

Jesus didn't hesitate but reached out and grabbed Peter's hand. "You of little faith," he chided Peter. "What happened, why did you doubt me?"

Peter's fleeting role as Braveheart was kaput.

Background

The disciples were obeying Jesus, crossing the Sea of Galilee in their fishing boat. It wasn't as if they had abandoned their rabbi and slipped off to a pool hall. Yet, they soon found themselves in trouble. As night fell and the storm picked up, they were fighting powerful waves to keep their small craft afloat. These sturdy fishermen feared for their lives.

Have you ever been surprised by trouble while trying to follow God? Sounds unfair, right? Don't be misled by pop theology that godly living makes one healthy, wealthy, and wise! That's not biblical, and it's a dangerous lie that can separate you from God. The Bible doesn't promise us blue skies. Or wine and roses. In fact, *Psalms* 34:19 tells us the opposite: "The good man does not escape all troubles—he has them too. But the Lord helps him in each and every one." *Psalms* 23 verifies this same promise: "Lo, though I pass through the valley of the shadow of death, I shall fear no evil, for thou art with me, thy rod and thy staff they comfort me."

It's true, believers are not immune from trials. They're not handing out free passes at the altar. But, it's equally true that God is an ever-present help in times of trouble.

Remember that Jesus had climbed a mountain to pray, evening had come, and the boat was far out in a raging storm. Obviously, something is going on here beyond the normal. No naked eye could penetrate that darkness, storm, and distance. What the Lord was "seeing" was extra-terrestrial. How wonderful it is when the Lord appears in the midst of tragedy or trauma, speaking peace to our troubled spirits! Peter and the disciples learned a lot about their Rabbi in the midst of a storm.

Life Applications

No Free Passes

Years ago, I hunted wild game with a crossbow. One day while I was sitting up in a tree blind, snow began falling. "This is great! The deer will be restless and moving!" So, I waited.

The snow turned to sleet. "Even better—now they'll be moving even more." The deer had better sense—they stayed in their beds of straw and hunkered down. Finally, it dawned that while I was high up in a tree shivering and freezing, my sweet wife was at home sitting by the fireplace sipping hot coffee. It was time to admit defeat and slink home. But, by this time, the tree was covered by a thick coating of ice. If you've ever seen a cat chased up a tree by a dog—then trying to claw its way back down—you can picture the scene.

At this point, God and I had a very serious discussion. "Lord, I know this was a foolish thing to do, but, if you will help me get out of this tree without breaking my neck, I promise you'll never need to do it again!"

For reflection:
When have you acted foolishly, then asked God to bail you out?
What's been your experience—trouble-free or forced to live by faith?

God Speaks in the Storms

Years ago, I was driving back to college late one night. Exhausted, I apparently dozed off at the wheel. How far the car traveled with me asleep I have no way of knowing. Suddenly, I awoke with an electric jolt—pulling into my sister's driveway about a mile from my dorm. The only conclusion I could come up with: Dad had been praying for me—and God had been steering the car!

For reflection:
When have you been surprised by trouble?
Has God used unusual circumstances to speak to you?

Try the Impossible

When President John Kennedy boldly announced America would put a man on the moon, the world laughed in his face.

"Who do these Americans think they are?"

"Who is this Johnny-come-lately who's going to do what's never been done by human beings?"

"They must have forgotten the Tower of Babel and how God humbled its would-be builders."

On and on the naysayers prattled. Meanwhile, engineers and scientists went to work. Gradually public opinion began to waver, shifting as people caught that "impossible dream." Some even began praying for success.

The Russians who had shocked the world by putting Sputnik in orbit suddenly became alarmed, jumping headlong into what had become a race to the moon. Even skeptics were becoming half-believers.

Then, on that historic night, millions of earthlings were glued to their televisions watching in awe as Neil Armstrong exited the landing craft proclaiming, "That's one small step for America and one giant step for mankind!"

I remember waking Talisa, our youngest daughter, in the middle of the night so she could one day tell her children and grandchildren of that moment when man's age-old dream of leaving earth and soaring into space unfolded to everyone's amazement.

A little-known P.S. to this story is what happened 9 minutes after Armstrong uttered his famous words. Buzz Aldrin also stepped onto the surface of the moon. A Presbyterian, he had brought along communion, and he thanked God for the success of the mission and took communion. And thus, Buzz Aldrin ate the first meal on the moon. Upon return to earth, taking his words from the Psalms, he said, "When I consider the heavens, the work of thy fingers, the moon and the stars which thou hast ordained, what is man that thou art mindful of him?" For Aldrin, a humble servant of God, the incredible achievement did not speak to him of personal accomplishment but of spiritual wonder.

For reflection:
Are you bold enough to try impossible things for God?
When has bravado or ambition for yourself
sabotaged your good intentions?
When are you most like Peter?

A BOY WITH SEIZURES

(Gospel account in Matthew 17:14-20; Mark 9:14-29; Luke 9:37-43)

A man approached Jesus and knelt before him. "Lord, I beg you to have mercy on my son, for he's my only child. He's mentally deranged, possessed by a spirit that has robbed him of speech.

He has seizures and is suffering greatly. Whenever it seizes him, it throws him on the ground. He foams at the mouth, gnashes his teeth and becomes rigid. It has often thrown him into fire or water to kill him. I asked your disciples to drive out the spirit, but they could not. But, if you can do anything, take pity on us and help us."

"If I can?" replied Jesus. "Everything is possible for him who believes."

The boy's father exclaimed, "I do believe; help me overcome my unbelief."

Turning to his disciples, Jesus said, "O, you stubborn and faithless people! How long must I put up with you? Bring the boy to me."

Background

After his disciples failed to help the boy, his father approached Jesus. The disciples' faith at this point was embryonic. They apparently forgot to seek God's help—and failed miserably. In today's world, too, our faith is often embryonic—and we often forget to ask God's help, trying to go it alone. However, when we ask, the miracles appear, as they did with the boy with seizures.

What else can we learn from this miracle? What about the man's candor? He admitted belief mixed with doubt. He asked Jesus to help if he could, and Jesus gave him everything he needed for his son. It is safe to tell

God what's in our heart. He knows it, anyway, and is touched by humble honesty. And, as this father discovered, God honors faith—even when it's mixed with doubt—and gives the maximum in response. As Jesus told his disciples after he was able to heal the child that they could not, even faith the size of a mustard seed can move mountains.

Life Applications

Use Your Faith: Ask God For Help

Once, a supervisor had to move someone who worked for her into a new department. Roger (not his real name) did not want to be transferred, but there was no choice. The requirement came from higher headquarters. The supervisor talked to him at length. She even took a half-hour walk around the office building, in the fresh air, using her most persuasive skills to answer his objections, explain why the move was required, how he would not be harmed by it, and more. As a task-oriented manager, she focused on all the important mission-oriented objectives and expected him to do so also. At the end of his last day before transferring, a Friday, he left an envelope with the supervisor's secretary. It was a personal note that he had somehow obtained that revealed some very personal and embarrassing information. He promised to keep the information to himself as long as he was not transferred. Clearly, the supervisor's power of persuasion had not swayed Roger. Operating on her own, she had failed miserably. Like the disciples, she had forgotten to seek God's help. She knew what she had to do!

Before Mass on Sunday, she asked God to provide an answer for her in the readings or homily. However, nothing obvious came up in the readings. So, she waited patiently for the homily. Surely, God would provide the answer in the homily. But, no. In fact, the homily was very short because the priest had difficulty speaking. He had arrived back in the United States from Colombia where he had been ill with bronchitis—and was still suffering from the ailment. Breathing and speaking pained him.

The supervisor had no answer about my work problem, but she did know a natural cure for bronchitis, given to me by the Siberians years earlier: inhalation of eucalyptus oil. So, she waited to be last in line to say goodbye to the priest after Mass and told him about eucalyptus oil. He promised to try it. (He did; it worked.)

As she walked to her car, the supervisor felt very disappointed that God had not given her an answer to her work problem though there was some satisfaction in His using her to help the priest. Then, suddenly, all became clear. Using her to help the priest *was* the answer to her work situation. Just as nothing in the homily was about her, just as the priest's need for eucalyptus oil was not about her, so she suddenly understood that the problem at work was also not about her. It was about Roger. She had focused on persuasion, not on listening. On Monday, she returned to work, listened to Roger, took his concerns seriously, and, as a result, Roger agreed to transfer, considering that she did have his interests at heart, as well as those of higher headquarters.

God is very clever in *how* he goes about helping us. How much easier everything is when we ask for the help we need—and trust God to provide it, as the supervisor found out.

For reflection:
What difference has faith made in your daily life?
Can you relate to the man's plea to Jesus,
"Lord, I believe but help my unbelief?"
When have you struggled with a mixture of faith and doubts?
When have you trusted in yourself when you
should have been turning to God for help?

Ask in Spite of Your Doubts—And Trust God to Over-Respond

A true story related to me by a friend confirms this. Here is her story as related to me:

"Years ago, I was conducting research in a small village (*selo*) of about eight families on the edge of Lake Pestova about two hours outside Moscow, Russia. No one had a car, except for one well-to-do businessman, Evgeny, who owned the only villa in the *selo*, whose rooms he rented out to people like me: international scholars conducting research on language and culture of the area. Evgeny did not live at the villa, so the car was available only during day time hours.

One night after midnight, I felt a terrible abdominal pain that I recognized as a very bad urinary infection that was in the process of shutting down her bladder. This had happened to me in the past, resulting in emergency room treatment, but there was no emergency room, no hospital, no ambulance, and until noon, not even a car. I managed to squeeze out the last of any urine I could manage, collecting in it in a bottle for a doctor when it would be possible to be transported to the hospital. It did look clearly infected. As time ticked on, the pain became unbearable. I tried to sleep; no luck.

So, I prayed. Not for what I wanted, but for what I thought I could get. Faith mixed with doubt? I asked for greater tolerance of pain. I did not tell God that I had doubt about asking for the infection to go away all by itself. My scientific brain told me that was not possible. So, I asked for what I thought was possible, not fully trusting that the impossible could be possible with God.

Of course, God knew I had those doubts. Of course, he knew what I really wanted but did not ask for.

Almost immediately, I felt a warm touch on my stomach and simultaneously saw from bed level and below the bottom of a brown robe and feet in sandals, fear, or awe, kept me from looking up. At the same time, the touch was so warm and pain-numbing that I immediately slid into sleep. A long sleep.

I awoke with the light of the morning and realized that I was not in pain. Bless the Lord, I thought. He has given me incredible pain tolerance. I stood up. No pain. And, then, feeling an urge that should not have been there, I went into the bathroom and was able to empty my bladder, having the presence of mind to reach for another bottle so that the doctor could see how far the infection had progressed. To my astonishment, the morning sample was sunny-day clear. I looked at the bottle from the night before; cloudy as a roiled river delta!

My veneer of doubt led me to ask for tolerance of pain. God knew that I needed to be cured. He gave me the greater thing.

For reflection:
God loves to see faith rising up in his children—but he also makes room for our doubts. Have you in desperation prayed for God to help you in a seemingly impossible situation, believing and doubting at the same time? What was the result?

God Can Move Mountains; You Just Have to Have a Little Faith

This same friend, whose story is recounted above, has experienced several miraculous healings of herself and her children. She freely admits, though, that her faith is still miniscule. Yet, she has learned to use it anyway. A little faith goes a long way—and she expects it to. She relies on the statement of Jesus that faith the size of a mustard seed will move mountains, and when she encounters a medical issue, she assumes that God will take care of it for her.

Another case in point is her experience with a torn rotator cuff. She had fallen down the stairs while moving boxes of books into a new house, and the local clinic took three x-rays of her throbbing shoulder. "Torn rotator cuff," the doctor pronounced and made an appointment for her to see an orthopedic surgeon for assessment right away.

The orthopedic surgeon took two more x-rays. "Torn rotator cuff," he pronounced and made arrangements for a CT Scan the following week to determine the kind and extent of surgery needed.

That weekend she attended Sunday Mass with her severely mentally challenged son, as she typically does. She had difficulty moving her arm more than a few inches when she greeted people before Mass began and explained to the parishioners around her that she had a torn rotator cuff. It was not something she worried about; she knew God would take care of it one way or another. (After all, doctors are often the hands of God.)

During the eucharistic prayer, as she knelt, she felt a presence between her and her son and a warm touch on her shoulder. When she stood with the other parishioners to say the Lord's Prayer and afterward give the kiss of peace, she instinctively lifted her arm to hug a friend in the pew in front of her. They were both surprised to see the arm functioning normally when only a few minutes earlier, it had not functioned at all.

Curious, she asked her son, whose reduced intellectual functioning often allows him to be more open to spiritual phenomena, if they had been alone on the kneeler. "No, not 'lone," he replied in his broken language, "Jesus there."

The MRI the following week confirmed the healing. The orthopedic surgeon canceled the surgery and hurried her out of his office. Apparently, an unexplainable (to him) healing frightened him. On the other hand, witnessing a healing the way that the disciples and others had witnessed Jesus healing 'the boy with seizures, strengthened the faith of that church community.'

For reflection:
Do you have faith the size of a mustard size?
Have you seen any mountains moved?
Do you believe that faith alone can move mountains?
What would increase your faith?

MASS HEALINGS IN DECAPOLIS

(Gospel account in Matthew 15:29-31; Mark 7:31-37)

Jesus left Sidon, walking down to the Sea of Galilee and into the region of the Decapolis. Then he went up on a mountain and sat down. Great crowds came to him, bringing the lame, blind, crippled, mute, and many others. They laid them at Jesus feet and he healed every one of them.

Jesus needed more time to spread the good news, so he urged everyone to keep quiet about the miracles he was doing. But the more he tried to squelch the miracle stories, the more they spread. Really, how could they keep such sensational news to themselves?

Background

Have you ever tried to keep a secret and failed? When our youngest daughter Talisa was small, she would beg her sisters to tell her what they were giving their mom for Christmas. They knew she couldn't keep a secret, but she would plead and beg, "I promise not to tell!" Finally, against their better judgment, they would give in and tell her. You know what happened, right? She didn't want to tell, she tried not to tell—but it was impossible. She loved her mother very much, and she knew this gift would make her happy. No way could she keep it to herself. So, it was just a matter of time. Some things are simply too good to keep secret.

When Jesus sat down on the mountaintop, he was "open for business." No internet, tweets, or twitters, yet the news traveled fast: Come quickly, Jesus of Nazareth is here! That set off a stampede. Soon people were bringing family and neighbors on crutches, mats, and donkeys to this charismatic healer.

In all the hullabaloo of so many healings, one man's victory might have gone unnoticed. Mark is the only gospel writer to record it. Here's what happened:

A deaf man with a speech impediment was brought to Jesus, and everyone begged him to lay his hands on the man and heal him. So, Jesus led him away from the crowd and put his fingers on the man's ears. Then, spitting on his own fingers, he touched the man's tongue. Looking up into heaven, he sighed loudly, and commanded, "Be opened!" Instantly the man could hear perfectly and speak plainly! Mark doesn't tell us why this man's story was singled out from all the other miracles our Lord did that day. Here's a possibility: It was a powerful way to convey Jesus' compassion. He loves people one by one. One needy human registers high on his Richter scale. Our God is concerned about every single person's need.

The Lord was fishing for people, strolling from one region to the next, attracting swarms of curious folks eager to hear him preach and heal. Jesus is still fishing for solitary souls. Our Lord's kindness was on display here as he ministered to God's hurting children. Everywhere he went, he found them wandering about aimlessly, disconsolate. The good news for us is, Jesus has not retired. He's still in business. If you're in trouble, you can depend on it—Jesus will seek you out.

Life Applications

You're Important to God

Kathryn Kuhlman, a famous evangelist of the 1900s, drew thousands to the world's largest auditoriums for miraculous healings. Wikipedia reports that two million people say they were healed in her crusades. She used screeners to interview those coming for healing, making sure they were not fakes or pretenders. Many of those cured are still alive today, offering their powerful stories as testimony that Jesus is still passing by.

Mathew tells us simply, "Then he went up on a mountainside and sat down." Have you noticed that no matter where he went, Jesus made himself accessible? No one was ignored or turned away. You may never be invited to the White House to chat with the President—or to the Vatican for a private audience with the Pope—but Jesus notices and cares for you.

The most bedraggled street urchin was welcomed. Prostitutes, drug addicts, jail birds, and even hated tax collectors he called friends. This drove the religious pooh-bahs nuts. And, if you open your heart to down-

and-outers, expect to be criticized. The good news is, you'll be continuing the Lord's work.

For reflection:
What does it mean to know you're so important to God?
How will that influence the way you treat others?

Jesus Will Seek You Out

Dr. Richard Halverson, when he was Chaplain of the United States Senate, invited me to join him for lunch in the Senate cafeteria. As we walked down the hall, we encountered an elevator operator, a Capitol police officer, and cafeteria workers. Dr. Halverson stopped to talk with each one, calling them by name and asking about their families or a prayer request they had shared with him. Later he explained, "I try to show them the same love and respect that I do the Senators."

For reflection:
Who are the forgotten ones Jesus would be drawn to today?
Who would you like to reach out to and befriend?

Are Such Things Still Happening?

You may believe the miracles of the Bible but doubt they're still happening in our scientific, sophisticated, and enlightened age. If so, consider Roger Baldwin's true story:

In the 1920s, my grandmother, Gertrude Lample, was diagnosed with tuberculosis. (Medical science had not yet found an effective treatment for TB.) She was in her late twenties and had four children under the age of ten. After her condition was confirmed and in the months following, her weight fell to about 80 pounds. The doctors offered her no hope.

Neither of my grandparents were Christians, but my grandmother's father was a born-again believer. At that time, he was a deacon of the Full Gospel Church of Baltimore, Maryland, formerly Christian Missionary Alliance Church. So, my great grandfather, James Clatchy, and the rest of the church deacons came to my grandmother's house to pray for her. When they went upstairs to pray, my grandfather being an unbeliever, remained downstairs.

As they were praying, my grandfather later said he felt the house begin to shake violently. My grandmother was instantly healed!

Because of this miracle, both my grandparents accepted Jesus as their personal Savior and lived for the Lord the rest of their lives. Grandmother went on to have seven more children and died when she was 69 years old.

When my grandparents died, only two of her ten children had accepted Christ as their personal Savior. (One of her children died at age two.) Although they didn't live to see the results of their many years of praying for their children, *every single one of them became believers!*

The Full Gospel Church later became Trinity Assembly of God, now located in Lutherville, Maryland. My brother, Dr. Earl Baldwin, served as Senior Pastor for 22 years, and I served as a Deacon for 30 years."

For reflection:
God is not dormant, or dead, or retired. And he's still doing wonders.
Have you or someone you know received a miracle?

THREE MIRACLES—JESUS ACCUSED OF SATANIC POWERS

(Gospel account in Matthew 9:27-38)

As Jesus walked along, two blind men followed him, shouting, "Son of David, have mercy on us!"

They even followed him into the house where he was staying. So, Jesus asked them, "Do you really believe I can make you see?"

"Yes, Lord," they told him, "we do."

He touched their eyes and told them, "Because of your faith, it will happen." Suddenly, their eyes opened and they could see.

Then, a man who'd been struck speechless by an evil spirit was brought to him. Jesus cast out the tormenting spirit. The man's tongue was released, and he began talking normally. The crowds were stunned. "Nothing like this has ever happened in Israel!" they exclaimed.

Background

Peter and the disciples were on a whirling merry-go-round, trying to follow their beloved teacher. Jesus was so unorthodox! They loved him, were enthused and infatuated, but many things they still didn't understand. To be fair, these were fishermen, day workers, and tax collectors, trying to understand the Son of God! Many times they must have despaired and wondered if they were up to the task. Of course, they were not. A huge part of their apprenticeship was learning they could do nothing on their own, but, anything was possible when they stayed connected to God's Fisherman.

The disciples finally found their destiny on the Day of Pentecost when the Holy Spirit filled the place where they were gathered. They had followed Jesus' command to wait in the city until they received the Holy Spirit. The Spirit was to be their helper, friend, guide, and guru. He would tell them where to go and when and how. What had been overwhelming became an exciting life-long adventure.

When he restored the two men's eyesight, Jesus warned the men sternly, "Don't tell anyone about this." Instead, they spread his fame all over the region.

Why the big secret? This was not the first time the Lord ordered people to zip their lips. Commentators tell us his concern was prompted by the antagonistic atmosphere prevailing against him in the Sanhedrin among Pharisees and Sadducees. These jealous, suspicious, conniving hypocrites saw Jesus as a threat to their power over the people. They would succeed in lynching him—but Jesus needed time to finish his mission on earth. He was buying time so that when Satan's hour came, our Redeemer could cry victoriously, "It is finished!"

When the demon was driven out and the mute man began speaking, the crowd was amazed, but the Pharisees threw cold water in their faces. "It's only by the prince of demons that he drives out demons," they sputtered.

They were accusing Jesus of partnering with Satan instead of with the Holy Spirit. Jesus warned them that blasphemy against the Holy Spirit is an unforgivable sin. So, the crowd was divided into two camps—those who believed what their eyes saw and those who stubbornly denied it.

Jesus didn't let unbelievers sabotage his ministry of reaching out to people and sickness. When he saw the people, he had compassion on them because they were harassed and helpless. That seems to be his marching orders for us.

You'll find the same reactions to Jesus today. If you tell everyone, "I'm okay, and you're okay" you will attract the crowds. Folks will slap you on the shoulder and call you "a jolly good fellow!" Telling people what they want to hear "tickles their ears" the Bible says. It makes them happy.

Telling people that Jesus came to atone for their sins implies criticism. That's not popular in a society that gives trophies for trying, for showing up, for being a good loser. So, some will embrace the gospel like manna from heaven. Others will convince themselves they don't need Jesus, that only weaklings need a crutch. Indeed, our Father has given us a free will to believe and be saved or to reject Jesus and face Judgment Day without a friend at court. He said to his disciples, "The harvest is plentiful, but the workers are few. Ask the Lord of the harvest, therefore, to send out more workers into his harvest field."

Why did Jesus keep reaching out to those rejecting him? Because he was reflecting his Father's heart. Spending an eternity separated from God is so unthinkable; therefore, he refuses to give up on us. He created us to be with him forever. He found no suitable companion in all the other wonderful creatures he formed.

Life Applications

How's Your Attitude?

How dependent are you on your eyes and tongue? How different our lives would be without them. Yet, often we take them for granted, presuming on God's favor.

Rick lost his voice to cancer of the tongue. He and his wife were teaching a divorce recovery class in our church at the time. Now, he communicates with the help of his loving wife Elaine and by using a pen and notebook when he's alone with others. Rick also communicates Christ's love to people by standing at the back of their church, shaking hands, and hugging people on their way out.

Rick prays each day, "Lord, I ask that the people I meet today will sense your peace, presence, and love. Father, pour your love all over me and then use me to today to share your love with others."

God has been faithful, giving Rick new ways to share the good news. He's asking Jesus to give him even more opportunities to serve and help others. Despite his handicaps, Rick practices an attitude of gratitude. As a result, he's filled with the joy of the Lord and brings the love of Jesus wherever he goes.

For reflection:
Rick has asked God to help him find new ways to minister.
Are you using your God-given situation to bless others?

Use Your Wounds to Help Others

By restoring their eyes and tongue, Jesus gave these men a second chance at life. Looking at these miracles, one is struck by how many damaged people the Lord restored and gave a second chance at life. Maybe it's happened to you.

Years ago, my wife Dot's eye was attacked by an unknown virus. Her eye swelled, turned an angry red, then white. We were frantic. At the time Dot was still a young woman, so the threat of losing her eye was terrifying both physically and psychologically. We cried out to God; our family and friends, church, even strangers began praying for her.

When we sought medical help, doctors found the virus almost impossible to diagnosis. The virus was displaying what the doctors called "atypical symptoms." Dot felt like a guinea pig as doctors surrounded her, calling in their interns to marvel at this rare disease.

She was examined in some of the nation's outstanding eye centers in Baltimore, Philadelphia, and Washington D.C.. Finally, she was accepted into a research protocol at the National Institutes of Health. Over several months, researchers finally isolated the virus and were able to treat and save her eye. How fortunate and grateful we were to her team of physicians! But, God was the ultimate source of her healing—and she gives him the glory.

For Dot, this beautiful praise song by Bill and Gloria Gaither says it best:

"He touched me, O, He touched me,
And O, the joy that fills my soul;
Something happened, and now I know,
He touched me and made me whole."

Have you been there—waiting in midnight darkness for God to touch you? In Dot's trial by fire, we learned not to presume on the precious gift of eyesight.

During this traumatic time, Bill Straub in our church took a personal interest in her battle. Every time he saw her he would come over, give her a hug, and want to know every detail, any sign of progress. And why was this good man so supportive, so concerned? Years earlier he'd lost an eye. His glass eye was so well matched to the color of his normal eye that it was hardly noticeable. After his traumatic battle, he would never again take his eyesight for granted—nor could he ignore other people in danger of losing theirs.

Celebrate Recovery is a Christ-based nationwide ministry to people in the grip of all kinds of addictions. One of the things that makes it so successful is that members divide into small groups battling the same addiction, then these groups work with counselors who have successfully overcome that specific problem.

Goodness knows our world is full of wounded warriors. People who fall and can't get up need a helping hand. Could you be one of God's wounded warriors, giving others the same affirmation God has given you?

For reflection:
Do you know someone struggling with issues you've encountered? How can you be an instrument God uses to touch them?

Following the Fisherman

In some churches, children are not allowed to sing "We're in the Lord's Army." It sounds too militaristic for their taste. These same people may be found marching in all kinds of political protests, but they're not about to march in God's Army.

One night, Dot dreamed she saw a huge line of people waiting to sign up for something. She asked someone in line, "What are you doing?"

The response came, "We're signing up for God's Army."

"Well, how do I to join?" she asked.

"Just get in line!" she was told. So, joyfully, she did.

Jesus is still sounding a call to arms. "The fields are ripe for harvest!" was a term the disciples understood. When grain is ripe, harvesters are urgently needed because they must act quickly. It was an opportunity not to be lost. Jesus urged his disciples to pray for more workers.

For reflection:
Do you believe people need the Lord? Why? Have you always believed that? If God asks, "Who shall I send to them?" will you say, "I'll go, send me"? What would it take for you to say that?

MIRACLE ON THE MOUNTAIN

(Gospel account in Matthew 17:1-13; Mark 9:2-13; Luke 9:28-36)

Jesus told his disciples, "Some of you standing here will not die until you see the Kingdom of God arrive in great power."

Sure enough, Peter, James, and John saw God reach down, clothe Jesus in glory, and bring two long dead saints back to earth to talk with him. Others saw Jesus resurrected and ascending back into heaven.

One day he took Peter, James, and John and climbed up a high mountain, where they were all alone. As he was praying, Jesus was transfigured. His face shone like the sun, and his clothes became dazzling white—as bright as a flash of lightening. Two men, Moses and Elijah, appeared and began talking with Jesus. They also were glorious to see. They were speaking about his coming departure and how he was going to fulfill God's plan by dying in Jerusalem. Peter, James, and John would soon be leading the Church on earth. As they watched, Jesus was transfigured from a lowly servant into the blinding white Lion of Judah, and long-dead prophets descended from heaven.

At this point in their trajectory, these future lions of the kingdom were newborn kittens. They needed to nail down their understanding of Jesus. He wasn't just another in a long line of charismatics. He was their long-awaited Messiah.

Peter said to Jesus, "Rabbi, it's good for us to be here. Let us put up three shelters—one for you, one for Moses, and one for Elijah." (Peter was so excited he didn't know what to say but felt he must say something! Have you been there?)

Bless Peter's heart, how often he put his foot and half a leg in his mouth! Maybe that's why it's easy for us to identify with him. Peter could make a bull in a china shop look like the Pope's Chief of Protocol! Yet, he became Jehovah's rock. Peter shows us what God can do to transform people like us—common earthen pots—into holy vessels. Filled with the Spirit, this blustery and blundering fisherman after Pentecost converted 3,000 people with a single sermon. People were healed by passing under his shadow.

Peter was thrilled to worship Moses, Elijah, and Jesus. While he was still sputtering, though, a bright cloud descended, and a thundering voice spoke, "This is my beloved Son, listen to him."

God the Father was correcting Peter, enlarging his understanding of his rabbi, helping him put all the pieces together. Before Jesus handed Peter the keys to the Kingdom of God, he must master Theology 101: Jesus and only Jesus is Lord of heaven and earth. Peter's zeal to worship needed a Holy Spirit adjustment. The Father was gently tutoring the little worship party on the mountain: He seemed to be coaching them, "Pay attention folks, you're willing and eager to worship—just be sure to direct your eyes to Jesus. Worship him!"

Background

On the final day before his crucifixion, Jesus was with his beloved disciples praying," Father, the time has come. Glorify your Son so he can give glory back to you. You have given him authority over everyone in all the earth. He gives eternal life to each one you have given him. And this is the way to have eternal life—to know you, the only true God, and Jesus Christ, the one you sent to earth. I brought glory to you here on earth by doing everything you told me to do. And now, Father, bring me into the glory we shared before the world began." (Selected passages from John 17)

High on the mountaintop, when God's glory fell upon Jesus, the Father was making it clear his Son is no ordinary man. Whatever differences we may have as Christians, one thing is non-negotiable: Jesus is Lord, the only begotten Son of God, and now the Resurrected Lamb of Glory! The Father glorified his Son. Now he's giving us that joyful opportunity.

We learn much from Peter—both good and bad. Do you identify with him? He knew something marvelous was happening on the mountain that day—he didn't quite understand what it was, but desperately wanted to be a part of it. You can almost see his mind-wheels turning, "Is this a sacred social visit with Moses and Elijah? Or maybe it's to be our private retreat." Eager Peter was ready to set up camp!

Talk about an unforgettable experience! As Peter, James, and John watched with open mouths, Jesus turned dazzling white. His face glowed so brightly they had to shield their eyes. Before they could regain their wits, Moses and Elijah appeared on the mountain, also clothed in Shekinah glory.

Apparently, they came to speak with Jesus about finishing well. Soon he'd be mobbed, beaten, hauled into kangaroo courts, victimized by false witnesses, convicted of nothing more than embarrassing the religious power brokers, scourged, and crucified. Oh, to have been a fly on the wall, listening in on this conversation!

While the Bible doesn't say so, Moses and Elijah were likely comforting our Lord in his final hours. You can imagine them encouraging Jesus, reminding him that his sacrificial death will open heaven's door to humanity.

Jesus, our Comforter, needed comforting. In his divinity he could pray, "Not my will but thine be done." In his humanity, he needed someone to hold his hand, to remind him this was the very plan he and his Father had conceived to recover their lost lambs, and victory was at hand.

From time to time, we all need a course correction, do we not? Something important is happening that we don't fully understand. We need discernment from the Holy Spirit, the one who leads us into all truth. God is delighted to do that for you. He will show you things that may astonish you. Don't panic. Stay calm. Focus on God, what you're hearing from him, and what he wants you to do next.

When God spoke from the cloud, the disciples were so terrified they threw themselves face down on the ground. Jesus came to them and touched them. "Get up. Don't be afraid!" So, they looked up and saw no one there but Jesus. The Lord sensed this was too much for his shocked troops to comprehend. He wanted to assure them they had nothing to fear from the Father. Take courage from this: His vision for you is glorious beyond your wildest dreams.

Life Applications

God Clarifies, Counsels, and Guides

Has God spoken to you in a dream or whispered to you about your future?

Many years ago a wonderful lady came into my life. I was not very spiritual, yet God broke through the fog and let me know she was to be my life companion. I cannot explain it except to say his silent voice was unmistakable. (It was sweeter still when she agreed!)

God is not playing hide and seek with you. He will pull back the curtain.

"Call upon me, and I will answer thee. I will show thee great and mighty things, hidden things, which thou knowest not." (Jeremiah 33:3 KJV)

For reflection:
Has the Holy Spirit given you clear guidance on a big decision?
How did the Holy Spirit do that?
Do you believe He will answer your important questions?

Recalculating, Recalculating!

Harry Howard never knew his real mother or father. Left at an orphanage at an early age, lost and overwhelmed, Harry was well fed and cared for but desperately wanted to belong to someone. His dreams came true when a wonderful Christian lady from Chicago came and took him home with her. In Sunday school, Harry learned all the childhood songs like, "Jesus loves me this I know". His life began to make sense. He decided to become a foreign missionary, and his adopted mother helped him get into Moody Bible Institute from which he graduated with honors.

Harry applied to several foreign mission boards but was found to have a health condition. This caused him to be rejected. Harry was devastated. What now? He had worked so hard for so long, feeling certain he was following God's will.

Meanwhile, Harry had gone back to his former orphanage and asked the president if he could teach a Bible study class. He was welcomed enthusiastically. The kids saw Harry as one of their own. He developed an immediate rapport with the children, becoming a confidant and friend of many.

"I labored there for 25 years, bringing hundreds of orphans to know the love of Jesus." Harry thought he knew God's plan, but the Lord had another idea. When Harry adjusted his dream to fit God's vision, he found it to be so much greater.

For reflection:
Have you ever experienced a situation like Harry's?

A Season for Listening

Our friend George Abbott, whose own miracle story is told elsewhere in this book, has shown us the miraculous power of listening. Blind since early childhood, George has trained himself to listen with incredible results. George lives just up the street from us. One Sunday morning we were to stop and take George to church with us. However, Dot must have been distracting me with her usual charm, so I absently-mindedly drove past the Abbotts' house without stopping. Finally, at the top of the hill, we remembered, turned around and drove back to his house. George was standing in his driveway smiling. Getting, in the car, he commented, "You almost forgot me, didn't you?" He had recognized the sound of our car in passing! On another day, when we picked George up he commented with a smile, "I didn't know you had bought new tires!" And, of course, he was right.

Counselors find listening to one another is often one of the key issues in troubled marriages. Parents and children find listening to each other is vitally important. Teachers spend countless hours repeating their instructions. Why do you suppose the bible is filled with repetition? And how often were his chosen people really listening. When Jesus admonished his listeners, "Let him who has ears listen", did he sound a bit frustrated?

Have you walked in Peter's shoes? Too often we feel we must say something when it would be far better to keep our lips zipped. The lovable old fisherman was teaching us—there's a season for listening.

For Reflection:
When have you missed the mark by failing to listen?
What can we learn from Peter's experience on the mountain that day?
(That God is willing to correct us if we will listen?)

THE WOMAN AT THE WELL

(Gospel account in John 4:1-42)

Some do not consider this encounter, recorded only in John's gospel, to be a miracle. As the story unfolds, you be the judge.

Jesus had left Judea, returning to Galilee. To get there, he was passing through Samaria. The power of the Holy Spirit was upon him. He came to a town called Sychar, near the field Jacob gave his son Joseph. Jacob's well was still there. Jesus, tired from the long hot walk, sat down by the well. It was around noon.

A Samaritan woman came to draw water. Jesus said to her, "Will you give me a drink?"

Jesus was hot, weary, and thirsty. Jacob's well just happened to be there when he needed it. This shady lady just happened to arrive at the well while Jesus was there—so many threads beautifully woven together to help a hurting wayfarer. They engaged in a conversation that led to her and a whole town learning that Jesus was their long awaited Messiah.

The woman was surprised when Jesus asked her for water, for Jews in those days refused to speak to Samaritans. "You're a Jew and I'm a Samaritan woman. Why are you asking me for a drink?"

Jesus replied, "If you only knew the gift God has for you and who I am, you would ask me, and I would give you living water."

The woman was still skeptical. "But sir, you don't even have a bucket to draw water, and this well is deep. So, how will you get this 'living water'? Besides, are you greater than Jacob our ancestor who gave us this well? How can you offer better water?"

Jesus replied, "People drinking this water soon become thirsty again. But anyone drinking the water I give will never thirst again. It becomes an artesian spring within them, giving them eternal life."

"Please sir, give me some of that water!" she pleaded.

Background

Jesus used Jacob's well to tell this pagan lady about God and his "living water." The lady was mystified and didn't quite understand Jesus' offer of living water.

Jesus decided it was time to engage the lady in a discussion about her lifestyle. "Go and get your husband." he told her.

"I don't have a husband." The woman replied.

Jesus said, "You're right; you don't have a husband. In fact, you've had five husbands, and you're not even married to the man you're living with now."

"Sir, you must be a prophet!"

Then, a strange thing happens. She asks Jesus a question about worshipping God. Do you detect the Holy Spirit guiding this conversation?

"So, tell me, why do you Jews insist that Jerusalem is the only place of worship while we Samaritans claim it's here at Mount Gerizim, where our ancestors worshipped?"

Jesus replied, "Believe me, the time is coming when it will no longer matter if you worship the Father here or in Jerusalem. The time is coming, and is already here, when true worshippers will worship the Father in spirit and in truth. The Father is looking for anyone who will worship him that way. For God is Spirit, and those who worship him must worship in spirit and truth."

The woman said, "Well, I know this much; the Messiah will come—the one called Christ. When he comes, he will explain everything to us."

Then Jesus told her, "I am the Messiah!"

The disciples came back and were astonished to find him talking to a woman—and a Samaritan woman at that! But they held their tongues. No one asked him why he was bothering with her or what they were discussing. But, their shock hung heavily in the air.

Why had their teacher violated hundreds of years of tradition? Why had he risked criticism and his own reputation? And to what purpose—was it worth the risk? Obviously, he was being guided by an inner compass. He sensed this lady was living a nightmare that needed to end. Here was an opportunity to salvage a wandering soul. Certainly, he realized the implications of getting involved. Yet, he plunged ahead.

The woman left with her heart on fire. In her excitement, she left her water jar at the well. Returning to her village, she told everyone, "Come and meet a man who told me everything I ever did! Can this be the Messiah?"

So, people came streaming from the village to meet him. What an unlikely choice she was for an evangelist! Small towns harbor few secrets. Her reputation was well known. Yet, she sounded the trumpet and started a pilgrimage.

What are the implications for us? God chooses whom he will. Never give up on anyone or count them out. Especially yourself. A famous evangelist said, "If God can use a nobody, he can use me!"

This lady didn't preach a sermon; she simply pointed people to Jesus. Smart on her part, would you agree? She could've blown it big time by coming on too strong. She didn't say, "I've found the Messiah!" Instead, she left the question hanging, "Could this be him?"

The villagers were swept up by the woman's enthusiasm. Many wanted to believe her. When they met Jesus, they begged him to stay for a visit in their town. So, he stayed on for two more days. That's all it took for many of them to hear his message and be convinced.

"Now we believe because we've heard him ourselves, not just because of what you told us." They told the woman. "He is indeed the Savior of the world."

They were willing to acknowledge Jesus but didn't want "that woman" to get much credit. People don't quickly forgive and forget. The good news is that a whole village was flooded with light. The woman didn't need everyone's applause; she had God's.

Most people don't like to be told what to believe. How about you? We'll listen to our parents and grandparents because they love us—and we know they're looking out for us. Beyond that, just give me the facts. I'll draw my own conclusions, thank you very much.

Sometimes an overly zealous new believer wants to grab people by the collar and shout in their face, "You're going straight to hell if you don't repent!" His theology may be sound, but his presentation could use some refining!

The woman at the well told them of meeting Jesus. They went and checked him out for themselves. How simple is that?

When the woman showed up to draw water just as Jesus sat down to rest, it seemed a coincidence. As we shall see, this was no mere chance happening. Her need was desperate, a deep heart thirst that well water couldn't quench. Jesus was meant to encounter this lady; she had a date with destiny. With God there are no coincidences.

Notice Jesus' patience with this bruised and fallen lady. He let her ramble on—and he listened. The Holy Spirit opened a door as Jesus listened. She began asking questions about worshipping God. Did you notice Jesus didn't tell her Samaritans were excluded? What can we learn from this brief encounter?

Life Applications

No Coincidences with God

George Abbott, our friend mentioned earlier, was struck totally blind as an infant. When he was a young boy, his mother and father dropped him off at a school for the blind, crying all the way back home. That heart-rending decision changed his life. George is an inspiration to everyone who knows him. He's successfully managed several small businesses for the blind, helping and inspiring countless people along the way.

For years, George set his alarm at 4:00 am, got up, dressed, and then walked with his cane nearly a mile to catch the Washington D.C. Metro to work. One day on a crowded subway platform, he was pushed and fell down inside the electrified tracks. Touching the super-hot electrified rail would be fatal. So would being run over by the next oncoming train. However, instead of dying, he was quickly pulled to safety by a good samaritan who risked his own life by jumping off the platform onto the tracks to rescue him.

"I allowed myself to be taken to the hospital but wasn't seriously hurt. As soon as my wounds healed, I forced myself to get up as usual, go down to the metro, and make a test run to my workplace. I knew if I didn't do it quickly, I would never have the courage to do it again!"

Ask George his secret, and he will point you to Jesus. "I've never gotten in a jam that he didn't send someone to help me. I could tell you one story after another. The Lord has always been there for me. He's never once let me down."

When God is leading and we're following, he lights our path. If you go with God's plan, you will be blessed—and you'll be a blessing. George will gladly tell you so.

For reflection:
Have you ever feared your circumstances? How did God use them for good?

People are Searching

Her name was Alice. She was in a small study group where participants were introducing themselves, telling something about their childhood. When it was Alice's turn, she spoke hesitantly.

"When I was a tiny little girl, I was put in an orphanage. I was not pretty at all, and no one wanted me. But I can recall longing to be adopted and loved by a family as far back as I can remember. I thought about it day and night, but everything I did seemed to go wrong. I tried too hard to please everyone who came to look me over, and all I did was drive people away.

Then one day the head of the orphanage told me a family was going to take me home with them. I was so excited I jumped up and down and cried. The matron reminded me that I was "on trial" and that it might not be a permanent arrangement. But I just knew it would be. So, I went with this family and started to school in their town—a very happy little girl. And life began to open up for me, just a little.

But one day, a few months later, I skipped home from school and ran in the front door of the big old house we lived in. No one was at home, but there in the middle of the front hall was my battered old suitcase with my little coat thrown over it. As I stood there and looked at that suitcase, it slowly dawned on me what it meant: they didn't want me. And I hadn't even suspected."

Alice stopped speaking for a moment. Then, she cleared her throat and said almost matter-of-factly, "That happened to me seven times before I was 13 years old."

Her companions looked at this tall 40-year-old woman and wept for her. She looked up, surprised and touched at what had happened to us as she shared her story. But she held up her hand and shook her head slightly in a gesture to stop us from feeling sorry for her. "Don't," she said with a genuinely happy smile, "I needed my past. You see—it brought me to God." (Living the Adventure, Keith Miller and Bruce Larson)

For reflection:
Like the woman at the well, Alice was searching.
Are you willing to help people like her find Jesus?
In what ways have you done this or prepared to do so?

Take Time to Listen

A couple is sitting in a romantic restaurant one evening, having dinner. The man keeps checking his cell phone messages and stopping to text his reply. When the lady has his attention, she tries to resume their conversation, only to be interrupted by his cell phone. You don't have to be a mind reader to sense how frustrated his companion is becoming.

The Stephens Ministry is a Christian group visiting the lonely, sick, and house-bound. The training program for this ministry stresses that what people often need more than anything else is someone to listen to them—listen to their "shaggy dog stories," the ones they keep repeating, trying to understand what makes this story so important to them, asking the Holy Spirit to give discernment.

For reflection:
When have you taken time to listen to people, letting them know they're worth your time? What kind of relationship developed from that? When have you failed to listen? Why? Would you handle the situation differently were you to have the opportunity?

A BLIND MAN AT BETHSAIDA

(Gospel account in Mark 8:22-26)

When Jesus arrived in Bethsaida, some people brought a blind man to him, begging the Lord to heal him. Jesus took him by the hand and led him out of the village. Then, he put spittle on the man's eyes and laid his hands on him, asking, "Do you see anything?"

The man looked around. "Yes." he said, "I see people, but not clearly. They look like trees walking around."

Jesus placed his hands over the man's eyes again. The man looked hard and realized this time his sight had been fully restored. Jesus sent him home seeing perfectly.

Background

Others brought the blind man to Jesus. Don't miss this essential link in the miracle. Someone cared. Someone went out of the way for him. Someone heard the Man of Miracles was passing by and thought, "If we can just get him to Jesus, he'll be healed."

The Bible is full of people helping people. Their names often remain unknown, but they're recorded in heaven. And Jesus remembers: "If you give even a cup of cold water to one of these, you're giving it to me."

Was this man important to Jesus? So important he interrupted his sermon to lead him out of the village for a private healing? Are you tuned-in or tuned-off to human needs? Do you see the God-given value in strangers? Most of us are sensitive to family and friends, maybe even co-workers and neighbors. But strangers? Not so much. Certainly, caution is wise. Scam artists and con men are on the prowl. Free handouts can become addictive. How does one know when to reach out, or when the risk to one's safety and security is too great?

"But," someone will say, "Jesus was filled with the Holy Spirit. He was led, guided, and protected by the Father." Exactly, and that's his dream for you. He has not left you to fend for yourself. When he gave his disciples the Great Commission, he added, "And remember, I am with you always, even to the end of the age!"

Besides, he warned us that if we try to save our life we'll end up losing it—but if we lose our life for his sake (to follow him) we'll save it. Strangers were important to Jesus. In fact, he willingly gave his life for them.

Life Applications

People Helping People

Americans are generous people. They give more to charities than any nation in the history of the world. Doesn't that bless your heart? What an encouragement that God isn't operating solo but gives us a part. You and I are surrounded with people trying to cope, needing a helping hand. God has put someone like that in your path. I don't know what your sweet spot is, but you have one. God gives each of us talents, resources, and life experiences to be used for good. Scripture tells us we're blessed because God loves us—and he wants to use us to bless others.

The youth group at our church each fall, usually in late November, piles into church busses going to rake the yards of seniors, handicapped, and others in the church family needing a helping hand. Their leaders will not allow them to accept payments or refreshments because they are being taught the Christian principle of giving, expecting nothing in return. What a wonderful witness to the neighbors when those busses pull up and two dozen teenagers go to work, raking and bagging leaves!

For reflection:
Can you think of one small thing you can do to brighten someone's day?

Followers with Aprons

Arlene Hawksford wore a servant's apron. Her heart was broken by the plight of Burmese refugees. She responded by inviting a college student to live with her family. She learned all she could about how the military dictators were killing and torturing dissidents.

Later, she took in an entire family of five into the basement of their tiny home. County health inspectors threatened to legally evict them for exceeding fire and safety codes. Arlene refused to be intimidated. The county backed down, unwilling to risk the adverse publicity of throwing these desperate people out on the cold streets.

Oh, for more apron-clad Christians! If you're an angel with an apron, you're an authentic follower of our Lord.

For reflection:
Why do you suppose a "servant heart" is so important to Jesus?

Persistence Pays Off

This story of the blind man shows us God does not always work in the same way. Maybe you've prayed and seen instant results. Or, maybe you've prayed for years over a loved one yet are still waiting.

One night I had a bizarre dream and awakened my wife laughing. "What's so funny?" Dot asked.

"Oh, I had this crazy dream. I was in a strange place and someone asked me, 'What's your name?' I told them, 'My name is Dogged Persistence.'"

"That's your whole name?" they asked.

"No, that's my first name. My last name is Pays Off."

Dot turned over and went back to sleep. Mercifully, she didn't have me committed! But, I still think God was telling me something.

People who work with alcohol and drug addicts face overwhelming odds. Missionaries often cope with burnout. Pastors may battle for years against declining attendance to keep their church doors open. God's kingdom work is never effortless. Yet, Jesus is on our team. To fight the good fight is our part. Knowing our efforts are pleasing to God is sufficient to keep us going.

For reflection:
How much persistence will you need to live a life of true signifiance?
How important is it to you knowing that you are part of a sacred regiment?

HOMETOWN MIRACLES

(Gospel account in Matthew 13:53-58; Mark 6:1-6; Luke 4:16-30)

Returning to his hometown, Jesus began teaching in their synagogue, and the people of Nazareth were amazed. But gossipers began planting doubts. Soon, they were circling Jesus like hens at a pecking party. "Where did this man get these things?" they asked. "What's this wisdom that's been given him and power to do miracles? Isn't this the carpenter's son? Isn't his mother's name Mary? (Haven't you heard the rumors about her?) Aren't his brothers James, Joseph, Judas, and Simon? Aren't his sisters here with us?" They worked themselves into a frenzy. "Who does he think he is?" And they took offense at him.

How could this local boy go from sawing boards and driving nails to healing the sick and raising the dead? Their minds locked out any such possibility. Are you surprised the locals were skeptical? Jesus' message was unorthodox. He didn't quote their revered rabbis but claimed to be hearing directly from God. His disciples were a ragtag bunch of former fishermen and a tax collector. So, they rejected him. And because of their stubborn unbelief, he couldn't do any mighty miracles in his own hometown except to place his hands on a few people and heal them.

Background

Do you see how the so-called "wisdom of men" leads people astray? They were so caught up in their own ideas, logic, prejudices, and suspicions that God's truth was eclipsed.

Sadly, human nature hasn't improved in 2,000 years. What do you see on the evening news? In your morning paper? How receptive are the media to the Nazarene and his message? How open are your open-minded friends to Jesus?

It's no wonder Jesus' former playmates were awestruck when they saw him doing miracles. Even his teachings astonished them. There was a question begging to be asked: "Where did this guy get that kind of power?" A fair question would you not agree?

The answer was obvious—no mere man raises the dead. This kind of power rests in God alone. The One who gives us life is the only one who can restore it. Charlatans and pretenders come and go, claiming power over life and the grave. Cooks say, "The proof is in the pudding!"

Jesus once challenged the doubters, "If you won't believe my words, then believe because of the works you see me doing."

Again and again he said, "I can do nothing except by my Father." He was pointing them to the Source.

The villagers were eyewitnesses to history, but instead of rejoicing that they were seeing what no man had ever seen, hearing what none had ever heard, they let their lower instincts take over. They couldn't resist comparing their lives to his—they're barely eking out a living in a forgotten dust-bowl town while their childhood buddy is being greatly exalted. "That's just not fair!" you can almost hear them grousing.

Someone said, "Not all of us can ride in the parade. Somebody has to sit on the sidewalk cheering!" Will that be you?

The lesson for us is clear: We must guard against our lower human nature. God will help us if we let him. If we're not careful, we may fall victim to the "Nazareth Disease" and miss the miracle God has for us. So, grab a lawn chair and get ready to cheer.

Life Applications

Resisting Our Lower Instincts

America is a nation obsessed with politics, would you agree? Pick up a daily newspaper or turn on the evening news, and what do you get? An endless recounting, digest, and commentary of the President's agenda and the goings on in Congress. Moreover, it seems we're growing ever more partisan and contentious—unyielding in our opinions and unwilling to compromise one iota, trading insults and character assassinations, acting more like a kangaroo court than a nation under God. That's why former First Lady Barbara Bush's recent funeral service was so uplifting. For a brief moment, our nation paused to remember who we really are. Three living presidents from different political parties and our current First Lady paid their respects to a feisty lady who spoke her mind but earned the love and admiration of her fellow Americans.

For reflection:
Do you find it hard to applaud when friends surpass you (win the promotion you deserve, become more popular on the social circuit, get invited to more social affairs, or their kids win more honors than yours)?

Playing a Loser's Game

It's easy to see where the naysayers of Nazareth went wrong: They were comparing themselves to Jesus! How ridiculous was that? But, have you ever looked at a neighbor's new car, thinking "That would look nice in my driveway?" Or, feel a twinge when someone's new house is bigger and better than yours or when your friend has a fancier dress, a fatter paycheck, more applause, better recognition, or greater appreciation. Are we touching any hot buttons? Playing the comparison game is for losers. That would be yours truly.

Two friends and I play golf together, and we happen to be similarly "handicapped." After a while, we invited another friend to join us. This guy is a natural. He can go out once or twice a year and drive the ball straight down the fairway and putt like a pro. It drives us nuts! If he weren't such a wonderfully humble Christian, we wouldn't keep asking him to join us!

Playing the comparison game leads to disappointment, discouragement, and disillusionment. Why so? Because no matter how pretty or smart or strong you are, you're going to find someone prettier or smarter or stronger.

So, folks, let's not slide down that slippery slope. God created you to be a winner, period. You're the best you this world will ever see. Why not let well enough alone? His plan for you is magnificent. Don't fall in the Deceiver's trap and wind up frustrated, angry, or jealous. Be yourself. That's enough.

By the way Vernon, you're still welcome to next week's golf game!

Profiling People

The story of America's tragic history with Native Americans is a classic story of profiling. When the nation was searching for a place to put high-level radioactive waste, my superiors in Washington D.C. sent me to explain to State, local community, and Native American leaders why scientists were looking at their land as a possible disposal site. Not surprisingly, I was not welcomed with open arms. Tribal leaders, in particular, were not ready to hear, "I'm from the government, and I'm here to help you!"

One of them got in my face and declared, "If those trucks start rolling onto our reservation, this time we won't be packing bows and arrows, we'll be waiting for you with assault rifles!"

I quickly learned the United States has broken almost every treaty our presidents signed with the tribes. Our ancestors forcibly moved them from one desolate location to another, that they were deceived and abused by those supposedly sent to help them. I learned that gullible innocents who once trusted us were violated and taken advantage of repeatedly, dismissed as savages. They decided no white man can be trusted. In desperation, they declared war on those who were taking their homelands by force. All their resistance was to no avail.

Now backed into some of the country's remote waste lands, here was Uncle Sam again knocking on their door. Was it any wonder I was greeted with anger, frustration, and fear?

I took into account their suffering. I listened and treated them with respect, not responding to insults or personal attacks but honestly answering their questions. Slowly, a miracle emerged. Russell Jim, a respected leader of the Yakima Tribe in Washington State, learned that my mother had Cherokee blood in her ancestry and decided to come to my rescue. He told his people he trusted me and believed I was trying to level with them. He dubbed me "Gentle Ben." Over the next ten years I had the honor of working with them as their friend, a memory I will always cherish. They proved to be kindly souls of honor and integrity. Both of us learned to avoid profiling and that love never fails.

For reflection:
Have you had reason to change your mind
about people you once distrusted?
Where do you see people being unfairly profiled today?

AFTER JOHN'S BEHEADING

(Gospel accounts in Matthew 14:1-14; Mark 6:14-34; Luke 9:7-9)

King Herod arrested John the Baptist, bound him, and threw him into prison because John confronted him for stealing his own brother's wife. Then, at a drunken birthday party for the king, he was beguiled into beheading John and having his severed head presented on a platter to please his stolen wife and her glamorous daughter.

John's followers came and took his body and laid it in a tomb. Then they went and told Jesus. When Jesus heard what happened to his cousin John, the forerunner God brought into the world to announce the arrival of the Messiah, he was heartbroken. He slipped away by boat to a solitary place.

He needed time to pray and mourn over this great loss, but it was not to be. Getting wind of where he had gone, crowds followed him on foot from the surrounding towns. When Jesus landed and saw the large crowd, he had compassion on them. Then, he laid aside his own grief, welcomed them, spoke to them about the kingdom of God, and cured those who needed healing.

Background

A king became infatuated with another man's wife. Once conceived, his sin gave birth to a monstrous chain of events. His lust led him to betray his own brother. He forcibly took his brother's wife for his own pleasure. John the Baptist fearlessly rebuked him. This brought shame and disgrace to both the king and his stolen wife Herodias. The queen burned with shame and plotted vengeance. King Herod was on a fear and guilt driven merry-go-round and couldn't get off.

So, the guilty king and his evil bride doubled down. Instead of heeding John's rebuke, they chose to kill the messenger. You already know how that turned out.

"Tell him you want John's head chopped off and brought to you on a platter!" her mother whispered. The king sent his executioner to slice off the Baptist's head and bring it back to the girl.

Have you noticed when one tells a lie, he often has to tell more lies to cover it? Sin and lying run in the same bloodline. Once you start down that slippery path, it's not easy to stop. Toeholds are hard to find.

All of us go astray. But we still have a choice. We can repent and receive God's mercy or harden our hearts and face the consequences. Which sounds like the better choice?

God's Word is clear, sin leads to death. At his birthday party, a beautiful young girl performed a seductive dance for the inebriated Herod. He was so enthralled he vowed to give her anything she desired.

We know the rest of the story. Herod and his illegitimate wife were so enraged by John's criticism they murdered God's prophet. As far as we know, Herod and Herodias died in their sins. John's work was finished, Jesus' was just beginning.

Life Applications

Sin Consumes People

In the fall of 1994, the nation was shocked by a heartbreaking story on national television. Two little boys had been kidnapped in rural South Carolina. Their young mother told police that a black man in a stocking cap jumped into her car at a dark crossroads, ordered her out at gunpoint, and sped away with her sons, Michael, four, and Alex, fourteen months, as she fell to her knees on the highway, screaming in rage and terror.

The pale young woman blinked into a bank of television cameras, begging the heartless kidnapper and carjacker to look into his heart and return her stolen babies. "Whoever has my children, please, please bring them home where they belong. They are loved and missed more than any children in the world."

Then, apparently on the chance that her two young sons were watching, she sobbed, "I feel in my heart you're okay. And your Momma and

Daddy will be waiting for you when you get home. I put my faith in the Lord that He will bring them home to us."

People in her hometown of Union and surrounding towns began wearing yellow ribbons, packing local churches, and praying for a miracle. Mom went on TV again, "I can't imagine why anyone would want to do such a thing. It could only be the work of a sick and unstable person."

The truth turned out to be far more gruesome than Mom's story. Susan Smith had made up the whole lie. The 23-year-old textile mill worker had fallen in love with the mill owner's son. In her twisted mind, she thought the two little boys were keeping him from marrying her. In a wicked plot to salvage the failing love affair, she dressed her children in neat clothes, drove to the lake. and then parked her car on a steep boat ramp. She stepped out, released the hand brake, and let the car carry her children to their deaths by slow suffocation under the water. They were still strapped in their seats.

A diver who discovered their bodies in the almost black water said, "I had to put my light against the window and peer in. I was able to see a small hand pressed against the glass."

This story was captured for history by New York Times Pulitzer Prize winning reporter Rick Bragg in his memoir, *All Over but the Shoutin'* (1997).

For reflection:
Where have you personally witnessed sin destroying lives?
How can this tragic story possibly help us?

Responding to the Victims

An opioid crisis is ravaging America. The toll on families is enormous, overtaking alcohol, violent crime, and highway fatalities as the leading cause of death. Congress has been shocked into holding hearings. Big pharmaceutical companies making a fortune are squirming on the witness stand, trying to explain why millions of these dangerous pain-killing drugs are being shipped to small towns of a few hundred people. Doctors, pharmacists, and hospitals too often seem unwilling to acknowledge any responsibility. The president has declared it a national emergency, but who will lead the battle to put guilty perpetuators in jail—and to educate and convince the public that abusing such drugs is not worth the consequences certain to follow? Our dying brothers and sisters need miracle-workers like Nehemiah who rebuilt the walls of Jerusalem, leaders with the heart of Jesus and a vision from God. America needs an army.

True to the American spirit, armies are springing up in unexpected places. First responders are being trained and equipped in emergency intervention techniques to save victims dying of overdoses. Libraries in hard-hit communities are taking up the battle, training staff to recognize overdoses, providing them with intervention techniques, and equipping them with life-saving medications and emergency equipment. Public schools are offering dramatic films and documentaries to warn young people of the dangers of drug abuse and providing them with clear teachings on how to avoid danger. Even in this dark hour, a thousand lights are flickering, giving victims and their families one more chance at life.

For reflection:
Do you know anyone caught up in this present danger?
What could you possibly do to help them?

Seasons of Grief Can Be Stepping-Stones

Sometimes people expect more than we can give. They come to us at inconvenient times. Maybe when we're broken ourselves. Yet, this remarkable story may have your name written on it. When we suffer the loss of a loved one, Jesus understands what we're going through—because he's been there. Our High Priest was a man of sorrows, acquainted with grief.

We may find our seasons of grief interrupted by the needs of a hurting world. Sometimes, God calls us to bind up our wounds, put our sorrows on hold, and reach out to comfort others. In fact, such a selfless sacrifice may speed your own recovery. The Bible puts it neatly, "God comforts us so that we may comfort others with the same comfort he has given us."

Sharleen Dluzak lost all four of her children to a rare genetic disease. She and her husband Rick had moved from California to Maryland to get the two older boys accepted into a nation-wide research program being conducted by the National Institutes of Health. Soon after arriving in Maryland, Shar found she was pregnant again, this time with twins. Tragically, they were born premature and died soon afterward. Shar, a dedicated Christian, had family and friends, their church, prayer groups, and people all over the country storming heaven to save the two older boys, yet God also called them home. Miraculously, through it all with God's loving kindness and support of the Holy Spirit, Shar held on to her faith, drawing even closer to Jesus. As soon as her deep heart wounds began healing, she threw her whole life into counseling, sharing, and praying for others dealing with all kinds of grief and personal struggles. Can you imagine what a comfort and inspiration it would be to have a brother or sister who passed through such indescribable pain, praying for you?

For reflection:
What helps you get through seasons of grief?
When have you pushed past your own pain to comfort someone?

JESUS COMES TO GENNESARAT

(Gospel account in Matthew 14:34-36; Mark 6:53-56)

Jesus and his disciples crossed the Sea of Galilee to Gennesaret. As soon as they got out of the boat, people recognized Jesus. They ran through the whole region, shouting the news: "Jesus is here!"

People gathered up their sick and brought them to him—some on mats and stretchers. Everywhere he went—into villages, towns, and countryside—they placed the sick in marketplaces for Jesus to pass by. They begged him to let them touch even the edge of his robe, and all who did so were healed.

Background

The disciples were helping with logistics, becoming fishers of men. The merchants were opening up their stalls to lay the sick. Family, friends, and neighbors were organizing transport. Stay-at-homes were praying,

"Come quickly while Jesus is here!" Neighbors were spreading the news. Good people were working together, bringing needy ones to Jesus. Excited people in Gennesaret rushed to gather up loved ones. The news was out, "Jesus of Nazareth is coming our way!"

Jesus was heaven's foot soldier, tramping the dusty roads of Galilee, bringing good news, finding God's lost sheep, and urging them, "Turn from your sin, and turn to God, for the Kingdom of Heaven is near."

He healed every kind of malady. The report of his miracles spread far beyond Galilee's borders. Sick people were soon coming to be healed from as far away as Syria. Yet, Jesus didn't wait for hurting people to find him. He sought them out. Whatever their sickness or pain or if they were insane, possessed by demons, or paralyzed, he healed them all. Enormous crowds followed him wherever he went.

Every four years, our nation elects a President. Plans go into high gear for the Inauguration ceremony. People scramble to get bleacher seats or good viewing spots along the parade route. Only a lucky few will get close enough to get a good view. Don't even hint to the Secret Service you'd like to touch him! Not so with Jesus. He was approachable. People knew that, and they believed he could and would help them.

Have you noticed what a vital role faith plays in the miracles of Jesus? In this story, faith saw Jesus' boat docking in Gennesaret. Feet of faith ran to spread the news. Faith gathered up loved ones and laid them in places Jesus would pass. Merchants of faith moved their goods and produce to the back of their stalls to make room for the sick. Faith moved trembling hands to reach out and touch Jesus. Faith prayed and believed. Faith waited and expected. People's faith and God's love became powerful partners—a holy alliance.

They begged Jesus for a miracle, "Master, just let us touch you! Even the hem of your cloak!" You can almost hear their urgent pleas: "Jesus, Son of David, have mercy on me!"

As Jesus came to each one, family and friends often pressed in around them. The Bible speaks of praying with deep Spirit-filled groanings. Desperate people were lifting their heavy hearts to God. What a beautiful scene: desperate believers communing with the Holy Father, Holy Spirit, and Holy Son!

Life Applications

Jesus is Coming Your Way

Yusef, a teacher at a US government school sent a letter to the director of his division, Louise (not her real name), a few years ago, to say goodbye. Louise, his supervisor's supervisor's supervisor, was surprised by the personal content of the letter because typically she was too far removed from the teachers to know details of their daily lives. The letter said simply, "I want to thank you for your leadership and say goodbye to you. I am having by-pass heart surgery, and the doctor has estimated I have only a 3% chance to survive, because I have been undergoing chemotherapy for metastasized cancer. Please pray for me."

Given the mandated separation of church and state in government organizations, Louise could have prayed for Yusef herself and said nothing—

and, following regulations, perhaps should have. However, she decided to take a risk. She shared the letter with all 400 people in her divisions, writing, “If you have a belief system that allows you to honor Yusef’s request, please do so.”

Overnight, the division sprang into action, a prayer warrior division of Christians, Muslims, Jews, and others, all joining together to pester God to help Yusef. Cards were sent to him; post-surgery Yusef’s colleagues visited him every day.

Less than a month later, Louise walked past Yuself’s office on her way to a meeting. The door was open. Yusef was behind his desk!

Astonished, Louise entered the room and asked only “How?”

Yusef smiled broadly. “I just came back this morning,” he said. “The doctors are in shock. They said my recovery like this is medically impossible.”

After that, more than 400 people knew that Jesus still passes by with love and healing.

For reflection:
Jesus often asked “What do you want me to do for you?”
If you could ask one thing of Jesus, what would it be?

Seasons of Desperation

Paul Yates went through such a season of desperation: He said,

“I was in my late fifties. My business had failed; I was saddled with a mountain of debt, no money, and no prospects.

To avoid losing our house, we rented it out for five years and went to live with our oldest daughter. I managed to find a makeshift job outside my lifetime profession which was in the jewelry business and began selling home improvements for Sears.

The job required a lot of travel, meeting people in their homes. As I was driving from one appointment to another, tears would often be rolling down my face for no apparent reason. Looking back, I realize I was close to a nervous breakdown. And yes, God seemed very silent.

One day I came home after a long day on the road to be greeted by my wife with amazing news: “You received a call today from a Valerie Baxendale.”

Val had been in the youth group of my home church back in the northern part of the United Kingdom (UK). I had not heard from her in over 30 years.

Val was in a ladies' prayer group in the church she and her husband attended—when the Lord told her, "Pray for Paul Yates." The thought would not go away. Her husband, a retired pastor, urged her to try and locate me. She knew we had immigrated to the United States. She contacted my cousin who gave her our phone number—and in obedience to the prompting of the Holy Spirit, Val made the call.

Can you imagine what that call meant to me? I was in serious depression and at the lowest point in my life. Of course, my feelings had nothing to do with whether God was working in me or for me. Deep down I knew Jesus promised never to leave us or forsake us—and I still believed this promise. But he looked into my heart and saw desperation. He opened up a little window to show me he was still working in my life—that was my call from the UK.

In his love for us, God created the church universal where each member plays a part. When one hurts, another feels it. I was hurting. Our loving Father knew all about it and prompted a long-lost friend, 3,000 miles away, to pray for me.

Then, later that same week, a friend left a voice mail that he was praying for me, the first and only time he ever did that. Knowing others were also praying gave me strength and endurance for the journey.

Did things get better? Not right away, but being reminded that God was present gave me strength and hope. Eventually, I was offered a great job in my field of knowledge, and things completely turned around. The last ten years of my working life were a gift from heaven that enabled us to pay our debts, move back into our house, and live comfortably."

Val's incredible call, after 30 years and from another continent, shouted what Paul so desperately needed to hear: "You'll be OK, Jesus is still passing by."

For reflection:
How do you cope with seasons of desperation?
Will you search your heart for someone who needs such a call—
and make it?

Gennesaret Will Never be the Same

A small dusty town on the wrong side of the lake, as the British say of America, Gennesaret was "across the pond," like an old scenic highway the world passes by when the interstate arrives. Not a lot was happening there--kids growing up and leaving for brighter lights, jobs, opportunities, going away to school, and choosing not to come back. Their forgotten folks were left-behind and going nowhere.

"Daddy, are we famous?" Seven-year-old Libby was looking up into her father's eyes.

He was Dr. Joseph. M. Stowell who years later would become president of Moody Bible Institute in Chicago—but that was far into the future.

"At the time, I was pastoring a church in a small Midwestern town," Dr. Stowell recalled. "So, it didn't take me long to respond."

"No, honey," I assured her; "we're not famous at all."

She paused thoughtfully, and then with confidence and a touch of consternation, replied, "Well, we would be if more people knew about us!"

"Poor Libby," her father quipped, "only seven and already concerned with what people thought about us—whether or not we registered on the Richter scale of public opinion." (*Simply Jesus*, Joseph M. Stowell)

Nobody was famous in Gennesaret. Few knew they existed—until Jesus arrived! We're not told how many days Jesus ministered there. Bones were mended, sight and hearing returned, tormenting spirits driven out, incurables healed. It was a life-changing event for those healed, those helping, and those witnessing it. Lost souls were salvaged, bandaged, washed clean as snow, and recruited into God's Salvation Army.

Two thousand years later we're still talking about it, mesmerized by the magic and majesty of what happened there. Families hand the story down to sons and daughters. Babies in grandmothers' laps hear of it. Little ones learn of the day Jesus came. He came to their aid. He answered their prayers. None were turned away.

Faith travels down history's stair steps. New generations are reaching out to touch this divine healer who ministers to all humanity. Gennesaret will never be the same.

For Reflection:
What would you like Jesus to do in your community?
Would you like to be famous? Why or why not?

A BLIND AND MUTE MAN

(Gospel account in Matthew 12:22-37; Mark 3:20-30; Luke 11:14-26)

Jesus kept on trudging across Galilee, out into the country, through dusty towns and villages, telling people about God and his love for them. The disciples stuck close beside him, as did some women he had cured. One of these was Mary Magdalene from whom Jesus drove out seven demons.

Jesus entered a house and a crowd engulfed him so that he and his disciples were not even able to eat. When the family heard about this, they went to take charge of him, saying "He's out of his mind."

A blind and mute man, possessed by a demon, was brought to him. Jesus healed him so he could talk and see. When the Pharisees heard this, they declared, "It's only by Beelzebub, the Prince of Demons that this fellow drives out demons."

Background

No wonder Jesus was called a man of sorrows! You might think driving out demons, restoring a man's tongue and eyesight would be applauded. But, you'd be wrong. Neither his own family nor religious authorities welcomed this miracle. His family decided he was crazy. The Pharisees claimed he was Satan in the flesh. His boyhood playmates and neighbors took offense because a hometown boy surpassed them. They fanned their grievances with loose gossip, burning with jealousy, envy, suspicion, character assassination, and imagined insults. You can almost hear then saying, "You're trying to tell me this illegitimate son of Joseph the carpenter is our long-awaited Yushua? No way! Not now, not ever!" Sadly, the Bible tells us, "He came to his own but his own received him not."

Friend of Jesus, don't expect accolades or bouquets from society. Expect Bronx cheers instead. If you follow Jesus, you're going to make the in-crowd uncomfortable, maybe even incensed and dangerous to your health. You'll not fly with the jet set nor dance at their parties. In fact, people at the water cooler will stop swapping jokes when you pass by. Expect to be a punching bag for gossips, back-stabbers, social climbers, politicians, pundits, and pallbearers. (Sorry, I added that last one to tickle your ears!) If "polite society" wanted to put Jesus in the looney bin and claim he was in league with Beelzebub, what will they do with you? In a word, expect all hell to break out against you.

If you're the world's friend, you're no friend of God. That's an easy choice, right? Wrong, but it's a courageous one. Aspire to emulate Jesus: just keep loving and serving; get over the petty put-downs and move on. A pastor challenged his congregation: "If you were arrested for being a Christian, would there be enough evidence to convict you?"

The "evidence" against Jesus was growing. When Jesus healed the man struck blind and unable to talk, by driving out a tormenting spirit, people were astonished. "Could this be the Son of David? Maybe he is the Messiah!' they exclaimed. The evidence pointing to Jesus being "Messiah" was accumulating.

The "jury" was still out on Jesus. People were weighing the evidence. And the evidence that this man was indeed the biblically prophesied Messiah was powerfully convincing. Jesus would be tried in kangaroo courts. People would lie under oath. He would be declared innocent yet crucified anyway. But, if they were looking for evidence to charge Jesus with being Messiah, they needed to look no further. If being Messiah was a crime, Jesus was guilty!

The man in this story could've won a Biggest Loser contest. Hollywood would break a leg to feature him in a reality show. Dr. Phil would interview him, psychoanalyzing his problems.

Deaf and mute, possessed by an evil spirit, disillusioned, despondent, and discombobulated, this man was a mess! Yet, a few minutes with Jesus was all it took to free him. Completely healed, he was given a new life, new opportunities, restored to his family, occupation, friends, and community.

When people link up with the Lord, they connect to unlimited power. The one who heals them also restores those years the locusts have eaten. He forgives their sins and anoints them for fruitful service. He redeems them and welcomes them into eternity. With Jesus no solitary soul is helpless, no life hopeless. That's why it's so important to help the dysfunctional, disoriented, and distressed find their way back to God. Jesus is the missing link. After all, he came to heal the sick—and he's still making house calls!

Jesus answered his enemies and exposed their hypocrisy: "Every kingdom divided against itself will be ruined. If Satan drives out Satan, he's destroying himself. And what about your followers—are they also casting out evil spirits using demonic powers? But, if I am casting out demons by the Spirit of God, then the Kingdom of God has come to you."

Jesus then warned them against committing the unpardonable sin: "He who is not with me is against me, and he who does not gather with me scatters. And so, I tell you, every sin and blasphemy will be forgiven, except blasphemy against the Spirit. That sin will not be forgiven. Anyone who speaks a word against the Son of man will be forgiven but anyone who speaks a word against the Holy Spirit will not be forgiven, either in this world or in the world to come."

Don't miss the point: Jesus was casting out demons by God's Spirit. The Pharisees denial was serious enough, but giving glory to Satan for this miraculous healing blasphemed God.

Life Applications

When Hell Breaks Loose

The man in this miracle had been robbed of eyesight and hearing by the powers of evil, but God sent Jesus to restore what the enemy had stolen. Have you noticed that when all hell breaks loose in our world today God sends help—often from the most unlikely sources?

Lester Holt, popular anchor of NBC Nightly News, once grew concerned that he was seeing so much suffering, reporting it to the nation, then moving on to his next assignment without staying to help. "It seemed so unfair", he told Guidepost Magazine.

"I remember visiting Somalia, where thousands of people were dying of starvation in the midst of civil war. We flew in to cover the story...then it was time to move on. But nothing was worse than reporting from Haiti after its catastrophic earthquake, in which more than 200,000 people perished. Here was death on a scale I'd never seen before: mass graves....survivors living on the streets and desperate for food and water. My crew and I initially slept in tents. We had shelter and food. So many did not".

Lester's network offered counseling to any who needed it—which he gratefully accepted. "Of course, I prayed, but I needed to know that our work helped rather than hindered. The counselor I met with asked, 'What would have happened if you hadn't gone to Haiti?'

I thought back on all the donations people made and are still making. All those huge transport planes that landed at the airfield—delivering medicine, food, water, clothes. What if no one had reported the story? No one would know."

Lester realized, "This was my calling—to shine a light in dark places. To give a voice to the voiceless."

For Reflection:
Where have you seen the Spirit of Jesus arising from unexpected places?
Have you experienced the joy of helping your fellowman in a crisis?

Help Those You Can

God likely hasn't called you to heal the deaf or blind. He does, though, expect us to do what we can.

When Katrina destroyed my sister's home in Hattiesburg, MS, and Dot's brother's and sister's homes in nearby Petal, MS, the Salvation Army, the Red Cross, and Christian mission groups responded by bringing food and water to stranded people living in temporary housing. Since electrical power was cut off for weeks and many roads were impassable, they even delivered ice door to door to preserve perishable foods, asking shocked victims if they needed transportation help to get medical attention. Other volunteers worked day and night to clear debris from blocked roadways and to help people begin rebuilding or salvaging anything that was still usable. Neighbors were also looking out for each other, especially the elderly and handicapped.

Judy's Story

Daughter of a prominent minister, Judy Matthews grew up in the political atmosphere of Washington, D.C.

Judy was a precocious, rambunctious child. Adventurous and sometimes rebellious, her eyes caught the attention of boys. Judy fell in love with love. This caused her preacher-dad untold headaches and her mother to grow prematurely grey.

But from the first day she can remember, Judy also fell hopelessly in love with children. She dreamed of having a home full of screaming, laughing, tussling, and tumbling little ones. Judy's second love grew out of joyful attendance every time the doors of her father's church opened. Judy grew up singing in a family of singers. Her ringing alto voice was strong and clear.

Eventually, God smiled on her infatuation with urchins by giving her a kind, loving spouse who also loved kids. Carroll Matthews came into her life gifted with a powerful tenor voice—one that shook the church chandeliers every Christmas Eve when he sang, "O Holy Night". Judy and Carroll became anchors in the Twinbrook Baptist Church Choir; also sharing their music at weddings and funerals.

First love and only daughter Amy of the big brown eyes and sunshine smile also became a great singer. First son Chip brought new joy to their marriage, followed by Jonathan, giving Carroll and Chip the decisive vote in family pow-wows.

As the children grew, Judy soon found yet another door of opportunity beckoning. Their community was struggling to provide stable households for babies and small children in tragic situations. In many cases mothers and fathers had abandoned them or abused them due to their own broken lives. Drugs and alcohol addictions had robbed some parents of the ability to cope. Other parents had themselves grown up under violent or dysfunctional parents—and were sadly perpetuating the tragic failures on their own children. In desperate cases, Social Services were forced to rescue the victims and try to find safe havens for them—including temporary moms and dads while trying to help their parents recover.

Judy and Carroll talked and prayed about volunteering to become foster parents. Well, maybe Judy and Amy did most of the talking. They convinced Carroll this was God's calling, took the required training, and were certified by county social services.

Thus began many years of exciting adventures for Judy and Amy, plus challenges and headaches for Carroll and the boys as they opened their home to distressed and displaced babies and children. Many of those terrified ones came with physical bruises, injuries, and emotional scars.

Judy had truly found her God-given calling.

Today one may find Judy leading a group of volunteer singers, bringing hymns to four area nursing homes. Extra-large print song books are given to the residents who join in singing the old songs they grew up loving 50 or 75 year ago.

Judy acknowledges her body is talking to her, reminding her of hard years and high mileage. But her love for hurting people, needy ones, forgotten and lonely ones, is still young, strong and vibrant. Despite the hard blows life has dealt her, Judy's love and faith has sustained her—and inspires her to keep on giving. Judy is an unlikely and unheralded angel, still cooperating with God.

For Reflection:
What special skills could you bring to such a crisis?
Would you be inclined to volunteer in an emergency?
Have you had the opportunity to do so?

Words Never Die

The Civil War was arguably America's darkest hour. Brother against brother, father against son, mothers' hearts torn between loved ones on the battlefields killing each other. As the war ended, people were desperate for a ray of hope. That is when President Abraham Lincoln traveled by train from the White House to Gettysburg to bring one of the greatest messages ever given. His words jumpstarted a desperately needed healing and rebuilding process.

Lincoln's words live on. Even today, schoolchildren are memorizing the Gettysburg Address. A nation is still trying to live up to its vision and promise. Imagine for a moment what might have happened if the President had used this critical moment for partisan, personal, or political advantage.

For reflection:
When have you been hurt by untrue or thoughtless words?
When have you had cause to regret careless words?

A SEVERED EAR RESTORED

(Gospel account in Matthew 26:36-56; Mark 14:32-52; Luke 22:39-53; John 18:1-12)

One of the most tragic stories in Holy Scripture leads us to this miracle. Jesus' encounter with evil this time involved his own inner circle. One of his beloved disciples betrayed him into the hands of a lynch mob. "Then all his disciples deserted him and fled."

Filled with foreboding, Jesus had gone to the Mount of Olives to pray, his disciples following. On reaching the place he warned them, "Pray that you will not fall into temptation."

Jesus was preparing for his fateful encounter with evil the same way he faced each day of his life. Dreading his coming death, he needed to be alone with his Father. He left his disciples and went on a little further and fell on the ground, saying "Father, if you are willing, take this cup from me, yet not my will but yours be done."

Being in anguish, he prayed more earnestly, and his sweat was like drops of blood falling to the ground. An angel from heaven appeared to him and strengthened him.

Jesus returned to his disciples and found them sleeping. These were his adopted ones, chosen to carry his message to the ends of the earth; zonked out as he prayed and sweated blood, another shocking disappointment for the man of sorrows.

"Couldn't you stay awake and watch with me even one hour?" he asked Peter. "Keep alert and pray. Otherwise temptation will overpower you."

Peter loudly proclaimed his faithfulness. Jesus was not impressed and foretold, "Before the cock crows three times, you will deny me."

Again, he warned them all, "The spirit is willing but the flesh is weak." His prophetic words soon became a nightmare for Peter.

Twice more Jesus left the disciples, going out under the olive trees, praying for help to endure his coming torture and death. Returning a third time, he asked, "Are you still sleeping? Look, the time has come. The Son of Man is betrayed into the hands of sinners. Get up, let's go out to meet him. See, my betrayer is here."

Jesus was about to be victimized by his trusted friend. Even his disciples were shocked at the evil hiding among them. Judas rushed up and greeted Jesus with a kiss. Oh, the depravity of fallen man! A beloved disciple betrayed his Messiah for a few silver coins. His betrayer had arranged a signal with the lynch mob: "The one I kiss, that's the one—seize him." He went to Jesus and said, "Greetings, Rabbi!" and kissed him.

Jesus replied, "Friend, go ahead, and do what you came for."

The self-appointed posse stepped forward, seized Jesus and arrested him. Then, Peter drew a sword and struck Malchus, the high Priest's servant, cutting off his right ear.

But Jesus commanded, "No more of this!" Then, he touched the man's ear and restored it.

Jesus rebuked Peter, "Put your sword away! All who live by the sword will die by the sword. Shall I not drink the cup the Father has given me? Don't you realize I could call on my Father who would send legions of angels to defend me? But how then would the Scriptures be fulfilled that tell us it must happen this way?" Then, the soldiers along with their Jewish instigators bound Jesus tightly.

Background

When Peter chopped off the man's ear, he reacted naturally. He knew Jesus was being railroaded by those determined to kill him. It seemed only right to defend his beloved teacher. But, Jesus saw God's higher plan unfolding and yielded himself up willingly.

When Jesus picked up the man's severed ear and restored it, can you imagine the chills shooting up and down the spines of his arrestors? "Who is this we're about to kill?"

Peter, no doubt, was astonished at the Lord's response; he's trying to save his Rabbi's life but gets rebuked! "But Lord, don't you understand this vigilante gang is out to kill you?" One can almost hear Peter protesting. Of course, Jesus understood. He knew it from the beginning. In fact, he and the Father planned the whole thing. There would be no resisting, no self-defense.

Christ's command to love our enemies is a lifelong challenge. Evil presses in from all sides. Every day we see its ugly face, leering at us from the front pages, taunting us on the evening news. Violence, cruelty, senseless killings, brutal beheadings—even claiming they're doing God a favor! Do good to those who do evil to you, the Bible tells us. Pray for those who abuse you, violate you, torture you—it's a tall order, is it not?

"Vengeance is mine," says the Lord. "I will repay." O how hard it is to turn the other cheek and wait for God, but to love them? Lord help us! How can we ever get there—rise up to God's standard? We can't. That's why our Father in his wisdom sent Jesus to live in us. Only by the Spirit of Jesus indwelling us is such a miracle possible.

But the Lord is still in his holy temple, he still reigns from heaven. He closely watches everything that happens here on earth. He hates those loving violence. He will rain down fire and brimstone on the wicked and scorch them with his burning wind. For God is good, and he loves goodness; the godly shall see his face.

The disciples thought they were safe from temptation, that they were strong enough to stand firm. They had been tutored by the Great Teacher. They loved, respected, and worshipped him. Yet they had one long ordeal to overcome before they were ready to change the world.

They needed to learn how weak and powerless they were in their own strength. This final night with Jesus—when they all deserted him to save their own skin—was their graduate training. After Calvary and Pentecost, they would finally be able to renounce their will for God's. They would be God's army or nothing.

Life Applications

After We Fall, What Then?

Bob Pierce was called to preach at the tender age of 12. That same year his father died. Struggling with almost unbearable grief, Bob recalls, "From that time, I've sinned, I've quit, I've failed, I've stumbled, I've fallen, I've landed in the mud puddle and come out drenched with mud. But one thing has been true: God set me apart, and there's no way I could run away from God. I have tried." Not an auspicious beginning for a servant of the Living God, would you agree? Yet Bob Pierce went on to spread the Youth for Christ movement to Asia while Billy Graham was bringing it to Great

Britain. When he saw abandoned Korean children eating out of trash cans and sleeping under cardboard boxes, he wrote in his Bible, "Let my heart be broken by the things that break the heart of God."

Bob went on to found World Vision. Today, that organization feeds, clothes, shelters, medicates, and brings hope to millions of suffering people.

For reflection:
When have you been most aware of your own weakness? Have you failed someone? (Take heart, God redeems and restores.)
What did you do following the failure?

The Sin of Betrayal

Chuck Templeton was a famous pastor, serving one of Toronto's largest churches. Along with his close friend Billy Graham, they traveled around the USA, filling football stadiums in great crusades. He helped Graham found Youth for Christ in Canada. His charismatic ability to communicate the gospel put him in demand as a speaker on platforms all over America. So, Christians were shocked when this man of God suddenly left his church and renounced the faith he was so powerfully proclaiming.

Templeton went on to fame and fortune, managing two of Canada's best-known newspapers, gaining influence with the Canadian Broadcasting Company, even running for prime minister of the nation. He defended the most tragic decision a person could ever make in a book, "Farewell to God: My Reasons for Rejecting the Christian Faith."

Toward the end of his life, Templeton was asked by writer Lee Strobel how he now feels about Jesus. With tears in his eyes, he confessed, *"I... miss... Him!"*

Chuck died in 2001. His good friend Billy Graham recently left this earth, joyfully looking forward to heaven. What do you suppose Chuck Templeton was looking forward to?

For reflection:
What could possibly cause you to betray Christ?
What do you think made Peter so sure he would not?

Deserted, Abandoned, and Alone

Can you relate to Jesus in this tragic moment? Have you given your heart to someone who turned out to be a cad? Has a brother or sister betrayed you? Maybe a best friend abandoned you? Did a son or daughter desert you when you desperately needed them?

Joyce Meyer, best-selling author and world-renown speaker, tells a story from her early days of marriage.

"Every Sunday afternoon during football season Dave wanted to watch the games on television. If it was not football season, it was some other 'ball season.' Dave enjoyed it all, and I did not enjoy any of it. He liked anything that involved a bouncing ball and could easily get so caught up in some sports that he didn't even know I existed.

One time I stood right in front of him and said very clearly, "Dave, I don't feel well at all; I feel like I'm going to die."

Without raising his eyes from the television screen, he said, "Uh huh, that's nice, dear."

Joyce recalled how she would give up on getting Dave's attention, go to the back of the house, sit on the bathroom floor, and cry. The crisis was solved, Joyce recalls, "when I learned to trust the Lord and stop wallowing in self-pity." (*Battlefield of the Mind*, 1995)

Gradually, Dave became more balanced about watching every sporting event. Today, he travels all over the globe with Joyce, helping her and applauding her every victory.

Loneliness is a universal human condition. In this advanced society where text-messages, tweets, Facebook, LinkedIn, and electronic messages blitz the airwaves, do you sometimes feel left out? You can push a button and be instantly in touch. Yet, when you need someone, is that someone available? Would you agree, this in-touch generation is mostly out of touch, unreachable?

Jesus had seen it all coming. He said, "You will abandon me and leave me all alone, yet I will not be alone for my Father is with me."

That's a pretty safe prophesy for you and me. Sooner or later, we'll find ourselves deserted, abandoned, and alone. Thank God, Jesus marked the trail. Now, we know the way out of our dungeons back into his marvelous light.

For reflection:
When have you felt most deserted, abandoned, or alone?
Does identifying with our Lord's agony help you to cope?

THE MIRACLE OF THE CROSS

(Gospel account in Matthew 21: 12-13; Mark 11: 15-17; Luke 19:45-46; John 2:13-24)

When Jesus arose from death, he fulfilled a promise. God's prophets had often foretold it. When he chased the crooked merchants and moneychangers out of the Temple, the Jewish leaders demanded, "If you have this authority from God, show us a miracle to prove it."

Knowing they were plotting to kill him, Jesus replied, "All right, destroy this temple and in three days I will raise it up."

As the sun rose on that glorious Easter morning, so did the Son! Of all the miracles Jesus did here on earth, this one changed the course of human history.

Background

The Lord had prepared his disciples for his approaching death and resurrection, "The Son of Man will be crucified but after three days in the grave, he will rise again." But they didn't understand—or refused to go there.

Here we find Jesus going to Jerusalem to celebrate Passover. In the temple area merchants were selling cattle, sheep, and doves for sacrifices, overcharging the people who came to offer sacrifices. Crooked moneychangers were fleecing them a second time.

Jesus made a whip from ropes and chased the hucksters out, driving out their sheep and oxen. He overturned the money grubbers' tables, spilling their coins. Then he charged over to those selling doves, yelling at them, "Get these things out of here. Don't turn my Father's house into a den of thieves!"

Wow! What happened to the Sunday school Jesus-Meek-and-Mild?

Then, his disciples remembered this prophesy from the Scriptures: "Concern for God's House will be my undoing." The religious humbugs were furious. "What right have you to order them out?" they demanded. "If you have this authority from God, show us a miracle to prove it."

"All right," Jesus replied," "this is the miracle I will do for you: Destroy this temple, and in three days I will raise it up!"

"What!" they exclaimed. "It took forty-six years to build this temple, and you can do it in three days?" But by "this temple" he meant his body.

After he came back to life again, the disciples remembered his saying this and realized the Scripture he quoted really did refer to him, and it had all come true. Jesus' critics were incensed by his outrageous claims, but the people hung on his every word. And, many were convinced that he was indeed the Messiah. You can understand the skepticism of his critics, can you not? No one had ever made such preposterous claims as did this Nazarene carpenter:

"I am the Son of God." "No man comes to the Father except through me." "My father and I are one."

Such claims were blasphemy to Pharisees and Sadducees—punishable by death. He was telling them their theology of laws and regulations couldn't get them into heaven—it was puny, anemic, and insufficient. Their sins could be forgiven only by trusting in him. His words stung them like hornets. They reacted like Jesus was spitting in their faces.

Yet, was Jesus telling them the truth? And if his mind-boggling claims were true, they must either accept them or find themselves fighting God.

Sadly, they chose the latter. Jesus had been given all authority from God, which was exactly what his enemies were denying. He claimed to be the cornerstone the builders were rejecting—the firm foundation—chief architect of God's house. Their minds were racing but their eyes and ears were closed to these fantastic claims.

Easter morning answered every reasonable doubt regarding Christ's identity. God has spoken. Let the earth be still!

"Prove to us your authority is from God." taunted his insolent adversaries. Jesus accepted their challenge: "You want a miracle? All right, here's your miracle. When you tear down this temple, I will raise it back up in three days."

They had no clue what he meant. After the resurrection, his disciples remembered and understood he was speaking of his crucifixion. Were his enemies convinced—or were their eyes still blinded by fear and jealousy?

God is not hiding from people. He has no desire to keep Jesus identity hidden from agnostics or atheists or truth-seekers. He's willing to meet people more than half-way. All that's required is a sincere yearning. Maybe you believe in God yet still have doubts about Jesus. Doubting Thomas certainly did, and Jesus gladly accepted his challenge. Why wouldn't our heavenly father be pleased to find one of his sons or daughters seeking the truth?

But, has God done enough? Here's the way Paul sums it up: "So they will have no excuse (when they stand before God on Judgment Day). Yes, they knew about him all right, but they wouldn't admit it or worship him or even thank him for his daily care." (Romans 8:20b-21 TLB)

God gave us a free will—and our sovereign choice is sacred to him. So, we find this strange dynamic working: some refuse to believe even in the face of overwhelming evidence. Jesus told us plainly in his parable of Lazarus and the rich man: "Some will not believe even though a man rises from the dead."

So, what more could God do—other than force his will upon us? Force unbelievers to recant and worship him? Not a chance! God wants his people to love him without locking them in shackles.

We're fortunate to live in the latter days—in the shadow of the cross. Why so? Because we can look back on the incarnation when God came to live with his people—and die for them. We see the Father's whole salvation pageant unfolding—Jesus' teachings, his miracles, and his ministry to the down-and-out. We see him hanging on the cross, suffering a gruesome death to redeem us. We see his broken, tortured and destroyed body gently laid in a tomb with spices. We share in the joy of a glorious Easter morning as he arises from death. We're there by faith as the Resurrected Lord of Glory ascends back into heaven, victor over death and the grave. Finally, we thrill at his promise to come again to take us to be with him forever.

Someone may say, "That's the end of the story. What else is left to do?" Just this: the Resurrection of Jesus is good news only to those who hear and believe it. God in his infinite wisdom left the last page of the saga for us. We're given the honor of sharing his story with our generation.

The Bible warns that those rejecting the Resurrected One will be rejected. Does this touch your heart? Those denying our Lord, he will deny before the Father in heaven. Does this terrible possibility frighten you for unbelieving loved ones? But, those who hear and believe have already passed from death into everlasting life. Praise the Lord for entrusting a tiny part of his kingdom work to us.

Has God done enough to make himself known? The apostle Paul speaks to this question in his epistle to the Romans: "The truth about God is known to man instinctively, God has put this knowledge in their hearts. Since earliest times men have seen the earth and sky and all God made and have known of his existence and great eternal power." (Romans 1:19-20 TLB)

What else has God done to make himself known to his people? He sent us prophets and holy men and women to speak for him. He gave us the Holy Bible, his inspired Word. What else could God do to convince his wayward and wandering ones that he loves them? How about incarnating his only Son and sending him on a mission to earth? Charging and empowering him to leave his glory in heaven, come to earth as a servant, show us the way home, then die on a cross for our sins—and be raised back to life?

Was that enough? How about gifting us with faith we can't self-generate? Forgiving our sticky sins that we can't shake off?

How about taking Chuck Colson, former confidant to President Nixon and his chief hatchet man, from a prison cell—a man who'd violated his high position of trust, and transforming him into a famous prison minister bringing thousands of jail birds to Jesus?

Or finding Tom Tarrants, a Ku Klux Klan gunman filled with hate, sitting in a Mississippi prison cell on death row for shooting into the homes of Blacks, endangering the lives of women and children, and firebombing Jewish homes and synagogues—changing his heart, and turning him into a pastor of an interracial church in Washington, D.C.?

So, God has done his part. He's made himself known to all. In fact, he's made it so plain that it takes a big effort to push away the truth. And, the Resurrection makes it nearly impossible. The caveat is this: hearts must be open. Saul of Tarsus being a dramatic exception, God doesn't often break down locked doors but, he's willing to be tested.

Life Applications

Living in the Shadow of the Cross

People today are asking the same question as people in the first century, who was this man? Was he merely a great teacher or prophet? Or is he the Lamb of God who takes away the sins of the world?

To accept his preposterous claims undermined their revered theology—or so they thought. Yet Jesus told them, "I came not to destroy the law but to fulfill it." Sadly, the religious muckety-mucks loved their positions of power more than the truth. You might think with two centuries of perspective the claims of Jesus would no longer be in dispute. Wrong. Today people are still arguing, disputing, and disagreeing.

Yet, the Word of God leaves no doubt regarding his identity. So, what's the source of confusion? Are the claims of Christ too much of a stretch for our rational, scientific age? Maybe the claims of Christ are too life-changing—too transformational. Could it be, we're not sure if we want to be transformed?

Maybe we're like the little boy whose mother put him to bed saying, "Johnny, you've been naughty. When you say your prayers, ask God to change you into a better boy." Closing the door, Mom stayed near to eavesdrop. Johnny prayed, "Dear God, Mommy wants you to make me into a better boy. But if you can't do it, don't worry, because I'm having a lot of fun just as I am!"

Dr. George Zachariah is one of those rare ones who live in peace surpassing all their circumstances. Two decades ago he was struck down by a life-threatening disease called Guillain-Barre syndrome. Paralyzed from the neck down, George was put on a life support machine with little hope of surviving.

Years earlier, he had been given a vision that changed his life. Already a man of God, George's encounter with Jesus was so powerful that he consecrated it by wearing a wooden cross.

Hospitalized for six-months, his recovery was slow and painful, yet his heavenly visitor sustained him. George remembers, "I can truthfully say, I was never worried."

His mind, heart, and spirit were at peace. He knew God was restoring him to his family and his beloved calling—teaching college theology, philosophy, and psychology. After his vision, nothing seems to faze George.

Our friend George can tell you, it's because the spirit of Jesus is still passing by.

For reflection:
What threatens your peace? Financial worries? Family trials? Career crisis? Safety or health issues? Our nation's direction? Unknown future? To find peace in all circumstances—how is that even possible?

God is Willing to Reveal Himself

What of Mother Theresa's story? Was it miraculous that this tiny frail lady plucked thousands of poor and dying "untouchables" from the gutters of Calcutta? Abandoned orphans, newborn babies, elderly, and the sick were rescued. Was it by the Spirit of Christ that this saintly woman loved them, took them home with her, fed their hunger-bloated stomachs, medicated their dying bodies, and nurtured their wounded souls?

She restored the dignity that a sin-darkened world had stolen. She convinced them they were priceless to Christ who loved them and was redeeming them to live with him in eternity.

What few knew at the time is revealed in her letters to her confessor that were shared with the reading public by a priest, a long-time friend, after her death. In *Mother Theresa: Come Be My Light: The Private Writings of the Saint of Calcutta* (Kolodiejchuk, 2009), we learn of the way in which God revealed himself to Mother Theresa. As a young nun in the order of the Sisters of Loreta in 1946, Mother Theresa was taking a train from Calcutta to Darjeeling for an annual retreat. On that train ride, she says, Jesus grabbed hold of her heart and placed in it his love of people, souls, and the poor. During the next several weeks, she clearly sensed Jesus asking her to come be his light and revealing his sorrow at the neglect of the poor. These revelations inspired her to found the Missionaries of Charity and minister to the very poorest people of Calcutta, work she began in 1948.

One can see parallels between her story and the experience of Saul of Tarsus, whom Jesus converted through a blinding vision. Both accepted their call and became messengers of Jesus' love. Though they differed in their faith background, Saul being an atheist deeply entrenched in Jewish theology and Mother Theresa having already taken vows as a Roman Catholic nun, both became zealous seekers of souls for Christ, having received a revelation seared into their memory and their consciousness for all time.

For reflection:
Do you know of anyone who has had a Saul of Tarsus experience? Or a revelation similar to that of Mother Theresa?
How has Christ revealed himself to you?

Responding to the Resurrection

Lee Strobel, a confirmed atheist, was an editor for the *Chicago Tribune* newspaper when his wife shocked him by converting to Christianity. Taking it as an affront, Lee began a 2-year crusade to prove or disprove her faith. But, after interviewing leading Christian scholars and leaders, studying the Scriptures for himself, and examining all the evidence he could find, he became convinced, renounced atheism, and embraced Christ as Messiah. By the end of his quest for the truth, Lee explained, "it would take more faith to maintain my atheism than to become a Christian."

Today, Strobel is an internationally known Christian author, speaker and pastor. His book, *The Case for Christ,* first published in 1998, became a best-seller and continues after 20 years to be a popular read for skeptics and believers alike. Last year, Lee's story was made into a faith-based film of the same name, starring Mike Vogel as the sincere investigative reporter who used his investigative skills in an attempt to refute Christianity and ended up as a believer.

For reflection:
Why is it so hard for some to acknowledge Christ?
(Is it pride, intellect, stubbornness, procrastination, sin, fear?)
How can you help those still wrestling with doubts?

Concluding Thought

The secret of a victorious life depends not on whether your miracle arrives now or in heaven. The conquering life has everything to do with trusting and abiding in Jesus—fully loved, gently led, graciously used by his indwelling Holy Spirit.

Study Guide
Discussion Questions

WATER INTO WINE

Do you have a problem with this miracle? Why or why not?

Why was Jesus reluctant to do this first miracle?

What do you think changed his mind? "Dear woman, that's not our problem," Jesus replied. "My time has not yet come." (John 2:4 NLT)

What impact did this miracle have on his disciples and why? (John 2:11) Discuss the conversations they may have had about it. They seemed to be trying to decide if he was the long-awaited Messiah. How did you arrive at yours?

Do you think others in the wedding party were convinced of his identity by this miracle? Why or why not?

After the wedding, Jesus went down to Capernaum with his mother and brothers and his disciples to spend a few days with them. Why do you think he did this? What good might have come of it?

If God gave you the power to do one miracle, what might be your first choice? Explain your answer.

THE WOMAN WHO TOUCHED JESUS

What admirable qualities do you see in this woman? What can you surmise about her from this story that would make her a candidate for God's mercy? (Faith, courage, determination, desperation, love, resourcefulness?)

What is your reaction to Jesus' comment, "I know someone deliberately touched me, for I felt healing power go out from me"? (Luke 8:46)

How does this tender episode and wonderful miracle boost your own faith?

What does it tell you about the Lord (e.g., that Jesus is approachable, tender-hearted, listens to our woes, and feels our pains)?

Discuss the impact this miracle likely had on the large crowd pressing around Jesus.

Do you think her healing was permanent? Why or why not?

After being healed this precious lady could have slipped away quietly. Why do you think she came trembling and fell at the Lord's feet—and in the presence of all the people, confessed her story of why she touched him and how she had been instantly healed?

A MAN BORN BLIND

Have you ever looked at the misfortunes of someone and been tempted to wonder if they had done something to cause their own distress? What did you conclude and why?

Have you wondered if you've caused some of the bad things that have befallen you? How does this story help you sort it all out?

With Jesus, it seems that compassion was normally his first reaction to suffering. What's yours? (How would you describe your attitude toward those who are hurting and struggling?)

"We must quickly carry out the tasks assigned to us by the One who sent us," Jesus told his disciples. Do you feel a sense of urgency to complete your God-given tasks? Which ones do you sense have the shortest fuse—that must be done quickly or never?

In this story, the Pharisees refused to acknowledge an obvious miracle. They kept investigating and interrogating but getting the same answers. Have you ever learned something that you didn't welcome and didn't really even want to acknowledge—but that proved to be true despite your misgivings? How did you deal with it?

What do you think of the evasive but clever way the blind man's parents answered the Pharisees' questions? Have you ever been put in a "no-win" predicament—and how did you cope with it?

What is one life application principle you gleaned from this story?

INVALID AT BETHESDA POOL

Regarding the story of an angel coming down to the pool from time to time and disturbing the water so that the first person stepping into it afterwards was healed—do you think that was just a tradition or literally true? Explain your conclusion.

Why do you think Jesus asked the man if he would like to get well?

Discuss the likely reaction to this miracle by (a) the disciples, (b) the other sick people at Bethesda pool, and (c) the religious leaders.

Discuss the Lord's warning to the former invalid in John 5: 14b, "Now that you're well, don't keep on sinning as you did before or something even worse may happen to you." (a) What does this imply about his former life? (b) What was his future potential as an ambassador for Christ?

What were the two crimes Jesus was accused of by the Jewish leaders? (John 5: 18) What do you think were their real motives for harassing and condemning him?

Reflect on Jesus' response to his accusers: "The Son can do nothing by himself. He does only what he sees the Father doing…and the Son will do far more awesome miracles than this man's healing. He will even raise from the dead anyone he wants to, just as the Father does." If Jesus could do nothing by himself, what does this imply for us?

When, where, and how did Jesus fulfill this claim to do even greater things than this?

A GENTILE WOMAN'S CHILD

This lady who appealed to Jesus was not Jewish—in fact, she was born in Syrian Phoenicia, a Canaanite, one of Israel's most troublesome enemies. Who would you find it especially hard to help? (What national ancestry, race, or social customs are difficult for you to understand or accept?)

If someone you love needed help, would you go to extreme lengths—even to a hostile country or former "enemy" to plead for them? If someone outside your comfort zone asks you to help a desperate loved one, would you try to do so? Elaborate on your reasons.

Were you put off by Jesus' first words to this mom, "It's not right to take the children's bread and toss it to their dogs"? (Matthew 15:26) How do you relate the Lord's first response to the culture of that time and place?

What convinced Jesus to violate tradition to grant her request? What does this say to you regarding traditions and popular customs?

When and where have you seen God's mercy extending to people you might deem unworthy?

What does it mean to you that as a believer you've been "grafted" into God's family?

Where were you, theologically and spiritually, before this grafting took place?

HEALING BLIND BARTIMAEUS

"Rich man, poor man, beggar man, thief. Doctor, lawyer, Indian chief!"

This was a popular rhyme once chanted by kids playing games. Have you noticed that society tends to lump people into categories? As Jesus and his entourage were leaving Jericho, a blind man, Bartimaeus, was sitting by the roadside begging. Why do you think Jesus interrupted his missionary journey to minister to a beggar? How could this possibly apply to you?

When he heard the noisy crowd coming his way, Bartimaeus asked, "What's happening?" They told him, "Jesus of Nazareth is passing by." Try to put yourself in Bartimaeus' place—what emotions were triggered when he heard these words? Discuss the premise of this book, JESUS IS STILL PASSING BY. In what sense is this true today? What is the significance to you?

As Bartimaeus cried out to Jesus, the crowd tried to hush him up. "Be quiet!" they scolded him. But he shouted all the more, "Son of David, have mercy on me!" Why were they trying to silence this poor blind man? (What are the dynamics of what's going on here?) When have you seen desperate people being ignored, their voices squelched? What is our Christian responsibility in such a case? How was this story insightful for you?

"Call him over!" Jesus commanded. Suddenly the mood of the crowd shifted, turning to Bartimaeus' favor. "Cheer up! On your feet! He's calling for you." Now they're the blind man's cheerleaders. When have you seen public sentiment shift suddenly with the political winds? What does this tell you of human nature—and how could it one day affect you? What is the take away for monitoring your attitude?

Throwing his cloak aside, he jumped to his feet and came to Jesus. "What do you want me to do for you?" Jesus asked him. "Rabbi, I want to see," the blind man responded. "Go, your faith has healed you," Jesus told him. What impresses you most about this story? What does it teach us about who can count on God? What does it say about how we should treat one another?

What was it Jesus saw in this blind beggar that gave him true worth? What makes you valuable to God?

As soon as he received his sight, Bartimaeus followed Jesus down the road, praising God. What is the significance of this? How do you think this miracle impacted his faith and his future? How was the community affected? What do you find most encouraging in this story?

A WIDOW'S DEAD SON

Compare the plight of a widow today with one in Jesus' day. What issues would be the same ones she was forced to cope with and which ones would be different? (Social services, proximity to family, home care, respect for the elderly, etc.)

What is the most touching moment of this encounter for you, and why?

What do you glean from this story vis-à-vis God's love, mercy, and compassion? What sense of urgency does it convey to you about helping those with special needs?

How do you think it impacted this widow's faith? The son's? The funeral procession? The community? (Discuss how far it has traveled down the highway of history.)

Do you sense that God personally notices and cares when you're hurting? What scriptures have been particularly helpful in this regard?

How can this story help us when we're facing giants, mountains, and "impossibilities"?

Contrast a Christian's funeral with that of an unbeliever. (Hope and assurance of a glorious future vs. what?) Share a scriptural promise you hold on to at such a time as this.

LAZARUS RAISED FROM DEATH

Why didn't the disciples want Jesus to return to Bethany to help his sick friend? (John 11:18)

"Let's go too and die with him," Thomas said. What new insight does this give you about "Doubting Thomas"?

When they arrived in Bethany, Lazarus had been in his tomb four days. What was the significance of Jesus waiting four days to raise him back to life?

Discuss Martha's expression of faith in John 11:22. What new insight does this give you into Martha's faith and love for Jesus? Compare the devotion of the two sisters to Jesus. Compare her expression of faith to Peter's historic declaration, "You are the Son of the Living God!"

What new insight was Jesus giving Martha in John 11: 25-26: "I am the one who raises the dead and gives them life again. Anyone who believes in me, even though he dies like anyone else, shall live again. He is given eternal life for believing in me and shall never perish. Do you believe this, Martha?"

When the Lord saw Mary and the others weeping over Lazarus, a deep anger welled up in him and he was deeply troubled. (vs. 33) "Where have you put him?" he asked. When they told him, "Lord come and see," Jesus wept. He was still angry as he arrived at the tomb. (vs. 34, 38a) Why do you think Jesus was angry?

What were the Pharisees and high council's real reasons for deciding to kill Jesus? (vs. 46-57) Discuss Jesus' response to their plan to murder him: How did it affect his public ministry to the people? His remaining time with the disciples?

A WOMAN CRIPPLED EIGHTEEN YEARS

"Should not this woman, a daughter of Abraham, whom Satan has kept bound for eighteen long years, be set free on the Sabbath day from what bound her?" Jesus confronted the self-righteous humbugs accusing him of breaking the law by doing this good deed. Question: Do you think that all or most or some diseases are caused by Satan? Explain your conclusion.

Jesus exposed the hypocrisy of the Pharisees by asking them if they watered their ox or donkey on the Sabbath. What do you consider allowable and off-limits for the Sabbath? What do you see as examples of being overly legalistic?

What is the meaning of the Lord's parable of the tiny mustard seed growing into a giant tree? (Luke 13:18-19) How does it relate to our everyday Christian duties?

What is the point of his parable of the woman making yeast bread? (Luke 13:20-21)

What is the more important spiritual principle in Sabbath keeping—to honor God or to rest? Elaborate on your conclusion.

Jesus interrupted his message to heal this handicapped lady. What insight does this give you vis-à-vis how God expects you to take up your cross daily and follow him? Would you say sharing the gospel and responding to human needs are inseparable? Explain your rationale.

Do you still have questions for God when you see a good person suffering? How have you resolved this issue? Have you searched for helpful insights in the Bible (e.g. Job, Psalms, Proverbs)?

INSANE MAN IN A GRAVEYARD

When Jesus stepped ashore, he was met by an insane, demon-possessed man. How do you suppose the sick man knew Jesus was coming? Was their meeting a coincidence or a divine appointment? Explain your conclusions.

When he saw Jesus, he ran and fell on his knees at the Lord's feet. He shouted at the top of his voice, "What do you want with me, Jesus, Son of the Most High God? Swear to God that you won't torture me!" For Jesus had commanded him, "Come out of this man, you evil spirit!" Why was the demon panicking with fear?

The demonic man was so strong he broke the chains and irons authorities used to bind him. Why were they trying to confine him? What was the source of his super-human strength?

Jesus asked him, "What is your name?" He replied, "My name is Legion," he replied, "For we are many." Do you think Jesus knew this already? What might have been the point of forcing him to acknowledge it?

A large herd of pigs was feeding on a nearby hillside. The demons begged Jesus, "If you drive us out, send us into the pigs." He said to them, "Go!" So they came out and went into the pigs. The whole herd rushed down the steep bank, into the lake, and drowned. As a lover of animals, do you have a problem with this part of the story? Are people more important to God than animals? Why or why not?

Those who heard what happened and came from town out of curiosity, found the former insane man sitting there, dressed, and in his right mind. They were afraid and pleaded with Jesus to leave their region. Why do you think they were afraid and asked Jesus to leave? So Jesus got in the boat and left. Discuss what good could have been done by Jesus for the people in the surrounding community had fear not aborted his visit.

What life applications did you find in this miracle?

A SCREAMING DEMON IN THE SYNAGOGUE

Why was the demon so overwrought with Jesus that he started screaming at him? (Mark 1:23-24) Was it fear, guilt, hatred, anger, anxiety?

How did the Lord respond—what did he command the demon to do? And why?

Why do you suppose the demon obeyed immediately?

Why did the people conclude Jesus was bringing them a new religion? (vs. 27) In what ways were they right? In what ways was it the same?

News spread quickly of all Jesus was saying and doing. What kinds of things do your think people were saying about him?

What do you feel was the most important thing that happened in the synagogue that day—and why?

Have you ever been present at a worship event when it was loudly and deliberately disrupted? Do you think evil spirits were involved? Why or why not?

JESUS STOPS A STORM

Have you ever gone through a tornado, storm or hurricane? What emotions were you experiencing? Were you afraid? Did you ask God to protect you? What happened?

What do you see as the main teaching point of this episode for yourself?

If love is indeed stronger than fear, and if love never fails, did the disciples' fear mean they didn't love Jesus? Explain your conclusion.

When faith, hope, and love must compete with our human nature, what gives believers an upper hand?

What scriptural promises have helped you cope with and conquer fear and anxiety?

The disciples were terrified, and asked each other, "Who is this one that even the winds and waves obey him?" What are the possible answers to this question? Had you been in the boat, what would you have concluded?

Discuss how this shared experience with the Lord helped them grow and become stronger witnesses and servant-leaders.

PETER'S MOTHER-IN-LAW

When Jesus came into the house, he saw Peter's mother-in-law lying in bed with a fever. He went to her bedside, bent down over her and rebuked the fever. The fever left her, Jesus took her by the hand and helped her up. Share with your group any stories you know personally about where the Lord has come to one's bedside and spoken to them. Were they healed? Was it instantly or gradually? What encouraging words did the Lord give them?

Peter takes the lion's share of attention in this story, but does this mean he was more important that the other disciples? Explain your conclusion.

Why do you think his mother-in-law's name was not included in this story? What spiritual insights does this whole interaction give you about your heart and attitudes to your in-laws?

Her ministry was apparently homemaking, cooking, and serving her family. Have your group reflect on what they see as each member's ministry gifts.

What would you like to hear from God? How would you expect it to come?

How would you rate yourself as a person who gets involved in helping others? Where would you like to grow as a servant of Christ?

Describe your best perception of the Lord's tailor-made vision for you?

TEN LEPERS HEALED

"Jesus, Master, have pity on us," ten lepers were calling loudly to Jesus as he walked between Samaria and Galilee on his way to Jerusalem. When he met them, he said, "Go show yourselves to the priests." And as they went, they were cleansed. For discussion: Parse this sequence of events: (1) they called out to Jesus for help; (2) he told them what to do; (3) as they were obeying his command, they were all healed. What is the significance of this sequence?

God often involves us in our own recovery. When have you sensed God telling you to do something to contribute to your own restoration? How did that turn out?

What do you think the ten lepers had heard about Jesus? How would they likely have known of him?

One of them, when he saw he was healed, turned back, praising God in a loud voice. He threw himself on the ground at Jesus' feet, thanking him. And this man was a Samaritan. (The implication seems to be that the others who failed to come back were Jewish.) Have you been disappointed when you've gone out of your way to help someone, and they didn't even acknowledge your kindness? How did you feel? What is a Christ like response when this happens?

These lepers were so isolated they may have been wondering, "Has God forgotten or abandoned us?" What could cause you to wonder if the Lord has given up on you or has forgotten you or rejected you? How would you try to recover your faith and spiritual equilibrium?

"Were not all ten of you healed?" Jesus asked. "Where are the other nine?" Good question, is it not? Brainstorm with your group for possible answers to the Lord's query.

Do you consider yourself to be a thankful believer? How much of your daily prayer time do you routinely spend acknowledging God's blessings and thanking him for specific ones? Brainstorm with your group and come up with ideas to help each other grow in thankfulness.

MAN WITH A SHRIVELED HAND

When they saw Jesus heal the man's shriveled hand, how did the Pharisees respond? (Mark 3:6) What does that tell you about them? How did Jesus respond to their hatred and threats? (Matthew 12:15). What spiritual insights do you glean from the Lord's response?

How did Jesus expose their hypocrisy and shame them into silence?

Why were the officious Pharisees and stiff necked teachers of the law so intent on trapping Jesus for breaking the law? Were they sincere protectors of Israel's covenant with Jehovah or small people parading around in holy vestments? Explain your conclusion.

Jesus looked at them in anger, and deeply distressed by their stubborn hearts, said to the man, "Stretch out your hand." In your own words, what do you think Jesus saw in their "stubborn hearts"?

The self-appointed gatekeepers were so determined not to work on the Sabbath that Jesus once told them they were straining at gnats and swallowing camels. What do you think he meant to imply? How could that apply to you?

What things do you find permissible to do on the Sabbath, and what things would make you uncomfortable? What are the ground rules you use to decide if something is okay?

Which ones would you put in the "definitely out of bound" category? And why?

A PARALYZED MAN FORGIVEN AND HEALED

Some men brought to Jesus a paralyzed man lying on a stretcher. When he saw their faith, he said to the paralytic, "Take heart Son, your sins are forgiven." (Matthew 9:2) Why did the Lord forgive his sins before he healed him? Which was more important—and why?

How did the crowd react to this miracle? (Matthew 9:1-8, Mark 2-12, and Luke 5: 25-26) Do you think others were influenced to follow Jesus that day--why or why not?

What do you think the writers Matthew, Mark, and Luke meant by their report that Jesus saw their faith? What would have convinced you of their faith? What evidences of faith do you hope God sees in you?

When Jesus told the man his sins were forgiven, some of the lawyers muttered to themselves, "This fellow is blaspheming!" Knowing their thoughts, he challenged them face-to-face, "Why do you entertain such evil thoughts in your hearts?" Which is easier: to say, "Your sins are forgiven," or to say, "Get up and walk"?

How do you think it made them feel to know Jesus had read their minds? How would you answer his question to them? Explain your answer.

What do you think of his friends removing tiles from the rooftop to let the man down in front of Jesus? Would you have been so bold? What is the life application here for you?

Some churches and faith groups hold special healing meetings open to anyone asking for prayer. Would you consider going to one to seek healing for yourself—or to bring someone in need? Explain your reasoning.

FEEDING THE FIVE THOUSAND

As evening approached, the people following Jesus grew hungry. The disciples suggested, "Lord, send them back to their villages where they can find food." Was that a reasonable solution? Why do you think Jesus rejected it?

How would you have responded to Jesus answer, "They don't need to go away. You give them something to eat"?

What life lessons do you think he was teaching (a) the hungry crowd and (b) his disciples?

Let's give them a smidgeon of credit—the disciples scrounged around through the crowd, then Andrew reported back to Jesus. "Here is a boy with five small loaves and two small fish but how far will that go among so many?" What kinds of thoughts were the disciples likely having at this point? Were they still clueless or beginning to anticipate a miracle?

Jesus said, "Have the people sit down." He then took the loaves, gave thanks, and distributed to those seated as much as they wanted. He did the same with the fish. Discuss the likely thoughts and conservations of the crowd as the food kept on coming. Imagine together the long-term impact this had on their lives.

They all ate and were satisfied. At Jesus command, the disciples then gathered up twelve basketfuls of leftovers so nothing was wasted. What do you guess happened to these leftovers?
What practical life lessons do you see in this miracle story that can help you day-to-day? (God supplies all our needs, even more than we can imagine; the rivers of God are filled with water; he blesses us that we may bless others, etc.)

A BIG FISH STORY

Do you think Jesus had already decided to recruit Peter and Andrew as disciples before he borrowed their boat? Explain your conclusion.

What qualities did Jesus see in Peter that may have indicated his potential? (Loquacious, bold, big hearted?)

Why do you think Jesus picked mostly blue-collar working people rather than religious and well-educated ones as his disciples? What classes of people were the main focus of his message?

What do you think convinced the twelve chosen ones to accept Jesus' invitation, give up their vocations, and follow him?

When Jesus first called Peter, he simply said, "Follow me." After Peter denied him three times, the Resurrected Lord appeared to him, restored him, and told him again, "Follow me." What does the Lord's open hearted mercy and forgiveness mean to you as a struggling follower who slips, falters, doubts, and fails to live up to Jesus' standards?

If you sense Jesus calling you to seek out people needing to come back to God, receive redemption, and be reconciled to him, how will you respond and what will it entail?

Have you ever asked God for a sign to let you clearly know his will? If so, what happened? Is that even a permissible request? What happens if God doesn't send you a telegram? What are your options then?

THE CENTURION'S SERVANT

What are some reasons why Jesus might have refused to help this man? (Was it: that he was a Roman military officer, occupier of Israel, unbeliever, Gentile?)

Why were the Jewish elders asking Jesus to help him? (Luke 7:3-5)

Why did the centurion say, "Lord, I don't deserve to have you come under my roof"?

How did the Roman officer's authority relate to Jesus' power to heal his servant? (vs. 8)

What was it about the centurion's faith that amazed Jesus?

Why did Jesus say some outsiders (Gentiles) will be welcomed to eat with Abraham in heaven while some subjects of the Kingdom will be thrown out? (Was it: God looks at the heart; salvation is by faith, not birth; and faith without works is dead?)

How can this miracle be an encouragement to us when we're praying for someone? (When we're asking and believing God for a long-distance healing?)

A FIG TREE WITHERS AND DIES

Early in the morning, as he and the disciples were leaving Bethany, returning to Jerusalem, Jesus was hungry. Noticing a fig tree by the roadside, he went over to it expecting to pick some ripe figs for breakfast, but found none—nothing but leaves. Disappointed, he said to the tree, "May you never bear fruit again!" When have you had an opportunity to help someone but failed?

The fig tree showed promise, being in full leaf, no longer dormant from winter. Yet instead of ripening figs, Jesus found it barren. God blesses us with unique gifts. Where do you sense God is calling you to become involved but you've thus far been barren? (Dormant, unprepared, unwilling, or unavailable?)

So, the fig tree disappointed the hungry travelers. We live in a world of consequences. Can you think of anything you've done or failed to do that you would like to have that opportunity back again? Do you believe God will make that possible if you ask him? (Or give you a different one?)

The next morning, they passed the fig tree again and saw it withered from its roots. Peter remembered and said to Jesus, "Rabbi, look! The fig tree you cursed has withered!" Jesus then explained the spiritual meaning of what had happened. "Have faith in God. I tell you the truth, if anyone says to this mountain 'Go throw yourself in the sea,' and does not doubt in his heart but believes in his heart that what he says will happen, it will be done for him." What are the common-sense boundaries of this promise? Are you testing God on this promise and with what results?

The Lord then warned them of one of the most common obstacles to receiving answers to our prayers. "But, when you pray, first forgive anyone you're holding anything against, so the Father in heaven will forgive you of your sins." Do you take this teaching literally and seriously? Are you comfortable praying, "Father, forgive me of my trespasses as I forgive those who trespass against me"? When you find it impossible to forgive, how will you deal with that to reopen your channel into God's favor and blessings?

Jesus' words caused the fig tree to wither and die. What are the words you hope to hear someday from the Lord? Where do you see confirmation of God's authority over all creation?

Imagine the disciples standing in front of the withered tree, and marveling: "How did you do that?" What wonderful things about Jesus cause you to marvel? What are you still learning about him?

A MAN WITH DROPSY

One Sabbath, when Jesus went to the house of a prominent Pharisee, he was being carefully watched by jealous rivals hoping to trap him into breaking the law so they could destroy him. Question: Have you been in a job or place where people were watching your every move, trying to do you harm? How did you feel—and how did you cope with the danger?

When Jesus refused to be intimidated by the legal beagles but instead did what he knew to be right, what good came of his courage? (two obvious ones—he healed the man of a disabling disease and exposed his critics' black hearts)

What influence do you think this healing had on (a) the disciples, (b) the guests at the dinner party, (c) the surrounding community?

Invite any members of your group to share a time they were facing danger from people who wanted to do them harm, yet found the courage to do the right thing. And what were the consequences?

Jesus noticed people jockeying to get the places of honor at the table instead of choosing a lower one. He reminded them that he who exalts himself will be humbled and vice versa. In your experience is this a common problem for Christians? Elaborate.

In what areas of your life do you find it most challenging to put others ahead of yourself?

Critique yourself as a host or hostess regarding who you invite to your dinners or social events. (Do your actions meet Jesus' standard? Are you willing to reevaluate and try to arrange your social customs to bring them more in harmony with the Lord's message?)

JAIRUS' DAUGHTER RAISED

A ruler of the synagogue came and fell at Jesus' feet, pleading with him to come to his house because his only daughter, a girl of about twelve, was dying. What was this respected Jewish authority risking to come and prostrate himself before Jesus, pleading with him to save his daughter's life?

Brainstorm together how the miracle likely influenced the future life of this twelve-year-old girl.

How did Jairus manage to keep his faith when friends came and told him his daughter had died?

Jesus said to Jairus, "Don't be afraid; just believe and she will be healed." Discuss the competing emotions likely going through Jairus' mind and roiling his spirit as they continued down the road to his house.

Why did Jesus forbid the mourners to go in and witness the girl's raising but rather sent them out of the house?

After she died, Jesus told them, "Stop wailing, she is not dead but asleep." Why did they laugh at him? Discuss their likely response when Jesus took her by the hand and said, "My child, get up!" Then, when her spirit returned and she stood up.

What does this teach us about trusting the emotions of a crowd? Discuss the impact of this miracle on her family, friends, and the community.

A LEPER IN GALILEE

A man covered with leprosy came and fell on his knees before Jesus, begging, "Lord, if you're willing you can make me clean." Jesus reached out his hand and touched the man. "I am willing," he said. "Be clean!" And immediately the leprosy vanished. Discussion: Jesus made it a habit of rising early in the morning before his disciples were awake, and going out alone to be with God and pray. What difference have you discovered on those days you begin with prayer and those times you rush into your day—without spending time or even checking in with God?

Did you notice the man's uncertainty when he fell at Jesus' feet begging for a miracle: "If you're willing, you can make me clean"? Why might this leper have doubted Jesus' willingness? Has the accuser ever tried to convince you that you are not a candidate for God' help—that some great mistake or transgression has disqualified you? If so, how did you resolve your misgivings?

When Jesus reached out and touched the diseased man, what was he conveying to him? How long do you suppose it had been since anyone had dared touch him? Was this an important part of this miracle? Why or why not?

Everywhere Jesus went, he was bringing people the same good news: "God loves you!" He found a hundred ways to say it, but this central truth kept coming through loud and clear. Do you think God's love for us is the heart, mind, and soul of the gospel? If so, why so?

Jesus came to do his father's will and seemed to have no difficulty discerning it. Assuming you also want to follow God's plan for your life, what has been your experience in discovering each day where that path is leading you? When in doubt, what do you do to find answers?

Some have linked the physical disease of leprosy with the spiritual disease of sin that isolates one from God. What do you think of this analogy? What are the similarities and differences?

Why do you think Jesus ordered the man: "Don't' tell anyone (you're healed) but go show yourself to the priest and offer the sacrifices Moses commanded as a testimony to them"? Why was this a better approach? Why was this required of a former leper before being accepted back into the community?

A TOUR OF GALILEE

Finding value in people, everywhere Jesus went he sought out those others had forgotten, discounted, or counted out. When he looked up and saw Zacchaeus hiding in the sycamore tree, it may have been the first time anyone ever looked up to the dreaded little tax collector. Why do you think Jesus sought the undesirables and untouchables? In your world, who would you like to show special mercy and kindness?

Why doesn't someone help? In a world full of violence and victims, of poverty and prisons, of hospitals and nursing homes, invalids and shut-ins, why are these brothers and sisters so often alone and neglected? Her grandmother was reading three-year-old Kaitlyn the story of the Little Red Hen, who was working hard to feed her family and friends. When they all refused her pleas for someone to help her, Kaitlyn grew visibly troubled. "Nanny, why wouldn't anyone help the Little Red Hen?" she asked. She sat quietly for a moment in her grandmother's lap. Then with a child's forgiving heart, she reflected, "Well, I guess they were all just 'wewaxing.'" (her best effort to pronounce relaxing) Question: How are you responding to others' pleas for help? (Or are you just "wewaxing"?)

Where can you help? You may be willing to follow Jesus in his kingdom work but are unsure where to begin. Henry Blackaby, popular speaker and writer, suggests you look around you to see where God is at work and rush to join him. The Salvation Army and many other Christian charities seem to show up where people are most desperate. Where do you see God using people to alleviate suffering? Which one may be calling your name?

Jesus became the Motivator-In-Chief as large crowds followed him enthusiastically across the Decapolis, Jerusalem, Judea, and the region across the Jordan. What was it about this curious but little-known iterant Rabbi that motivated others to join his entourage? What initially aroused your interest in him? How has he motivated you?

Are you flying solo? Jesus said, "I am the vine, you are the branches. He who abides in me and I in him will bear much fruit. Apart from me you can do nothing." (John 15:5 paraphrased) In your own words, what does this teaching mean to you? Was he being melodramatic for emphasis—or did he literally mean we can accomplish nothing good apart from him? Explain your conclusion. What fruit are you bearing by abiding in him?

"O, Lord my God, many and many a time, you have done great miracles for us, and we are ever in your thoughts." (Psalm 40:5 TLB) What can you point to in your own life that you would consider to be a miracle from God?

What does the second part of the above scripture—that we are ever in his thoughts, mean to you? (Describe the sense of peace, the blessed assurance, the optimism—or other heart helps this brings to you.)

JESUS PAYS HIS TAXES

What do you see as the main point of this unique miracle?

Discuss and compare your philosophy toward paying taxes with your study group.

Some Christian sects believe all government is evil and thus refuse to pay their taxes. Discuss the implications of this and why they should be exempted—or why not?

Under what circumstances, if any, is it right for a Christian to disobey a law?

Maybe you've not caught a fish with money in its mouth, but can you think of a time when you received unexpected help in a difficult time? Do you think God was involved? Why or Why not?

Do you find it strange that Peter didn't question Jesus' suggested solution? What reasons can you think of that would explain why this professional fisherman would buy into such a way-out sounding plan?

Discuss the practical lessons—life applications for us.

JESUS WALKS ON WATER

After feeding the five thousand, Jesus saw they were ready to take him by force and make him king, so he went higher into the mountains alone. Why were the crowds so determined to make him King of the Jews? (To defeat Rome and end their military occupation? To usher in their concept of the Kingdom of God led by a conquering Messiah?)

Why do you think Jesus sent his disciples on ahead of him to Bethsaida on the other side of the Sea of Galilee? (He may have wanted a few moments alone with the people before sending them home; he needed to climb the mountain to have time alone with God, etc.)

When evening came and the disciples' boat was far from shore, a strong storm arose. From high on the mountain, Jesus saw them straining at their oars, trying to keep the boat from capsizing. How was it possible for Jesus to see them at night and at such a great distance and in the midst of a storm? (This was beyond the limits of normal human vision, so how do you explain it?)

How would you have responded to seeing Jesus walking on the stormy waves?

Why do you suppose Peter wanted to walk on the water? Why did Jesus agree?

In what sense did Peter succeed, and how did he fail in his attempt?

What did Peter learn from this miracle? The disciples? What did you learn that could have implications for your faith journey?

A SPEECHLESS BOY WITH SEIZURES

This father with wavering faith appealed to Jesus to heal his sick son. The boy was suffering life-threatening seizures caused by a tormenting spirit. "But if you can do anything, take pity on us and help us," the father pleaded. When the boy was being brought to Jesus, the demon threw him to the ground in a convulsion. But Jesus rebuked the evil spirit, healed the boy, and gave him back to his father. How does Jesus' willingness to heal the boy, despite his father's uncertainty, speak to you when your flame of faith is flickering?

The disciples were unable to heal the sick boy. Discuss how they must have felt when they failed. When does it mean to you that Jesus kept on loving them, refused to give up on them, and gave them crucial roles in his ministry?

When have you wondered if God could or would handle a seemingly impossible situation?

What does this story teach us about being candid with God but giving him the benefit of our doubts?

Jesus responded, "What do you mean, if I can? Anything is possible if you believe." Share a story you know of personally where this fairy tale sounding promise literally came true.

Do you need more faith? (Who doesn't?) James tells us that if we lack faith, let us ask God who gives generously. If you could have more faith in one area of your life, where would it be?

Remember Jesus' challenge to a doubting Thomas, who was struggling to believe the Lord had risen. He told Thomas to touch his pierced hands and side. When he had done so, Jesus told him, "Now, stop your doubting, and believe!" How can this story help you deal with seasons of uncertainty and doubts?

MASS HEALINGS IN DECAPOLIS

Jesus left the vicinity of Tyre, walking down to the Sea of Galilee and into the region of Decapolis. A passion burned deep within him for hurting people, those anchorless ones being cast to and fro, buffeted by the hard waves of life. Where do you sense Jesus is still seeking out those adrift in the maelstroms of life? How do his methods and approaches today differ from then?

Climbing up on a mountainside, he sat down. Great crowds came to him, bringing the lame, the blind, the crippled, the mute and many others, and laid them at his feet—and he healed them. Do you detect a pattern emerging here as to how needy ones are connected to the healing ministry of Jesus?

Since the Lord is not physically present today, what are some ways people can be brought into his orbit? How might you be involved?

Jesus apparently made himself available to all petitioners—personalizing God's open-door policy. What challenges might you encounter today in opening your life to all comers? What reasonable precautions would be wise?

How are churches today fulfilling or falling short of this universal appeal and acceptance?

Why do you think Jesus was drawn especially to the poor, widows, orphans, down-and-outers, and those barely clinging to the outer fringes of society? Was this fair to the rich, famous, and powerful? Why or why not?

How would you articulate this vision? What scriptures come to mind?

THREE MIRACLES—
JESUS ACCUSED OF USING SATANIC POWERS

Have you known a person who could not hear or could not speak? What difficulties did they have to cope with as a part of their everyday routine?

What special social services or accommodations are available today that were not provided to them? (Public transit access, handicapped ramps, in-home nursing care, food assistance etc.?)

How did their lives change physically, emotionally, mentally, and spiritually when Jesus restored their eyes and speech?

Why did Jesus first ask the blind men, "Do you believe I am able to do this?"

When the formerly mute man learned he could speak, what do you suppose were some of his first words? Who would he likely want to talk to first and why?

Why did the Pharisees attribute Jesus' healing power to the Prince of Demons?

Do you think they were guilty of blasphemy against the Holy Spirit? Why or why not?

MIRACLE ON THE MOUNTAIN: THE TRANSFIGURATION

On top of a mountain, Peter, James, and John saw God reach down to clothe Jesus in dazzling white glory and bring two long dead saints back to earth. What do you think was the point of this show-but-don't-tell transfiguration?

How might it have prepared them for their future leadership roles in the early church?

Every scripture is given for our edification, right? So, what spiritual insights do you glean from the transfiguration? (Be careful who you worship, Jesus is the beloved Son, loved by the Father, Listen to him etc.)

Would you surmise this unearthly encounter with Moses and Elijah encouraged and strengthened Jesus to face the agony of the cross? If so, how so?

Has God spoken to you in a dream or whispered to you about something in your future? Do you feel comfortable to share it?

Peter was rebuked by the Father for speaking when he should have been listening? Can you recall a time you fell into this trap? Are you comfortable to share it?

Peter needed a course correction. When has God helped you stop, think, look, and listen to get you back on track?

THE WOMAN AT THE WELL

How did Jesus know so much about her past?

Do you consider this encounter with the woman, her conversion, and the response of the village to be a miracle? Why or why not?

Jesus would have been following important Jewish tradition had he refused to speak to her—why do you think he chose to engage her in conversation?

Do you think she responded to Jesus by drawing water to quench his thirst? Why or why not? And why do you think this part was omitted in the scripture?

How did Jesus bring up the subject of her spiritual need? (John 4:10-14) What insights does this give you in trying to relate to unsaved loved ones?

What do you think of Jesus answer to her question about the right place to worship? (vs. 20-24) He refused to be distracted from her real need—how does that help you in sharing the good news?

What convinced the people to believe her story and conclude that Jesus is "indeed the Savior of the world"? (vs. 39-42) Discuss the Lord's teaching moment with the disciples afterward about harvesting souls. (vs. 35-38)

A BLIND MAN IN BETHSAIDA

Jesus put spittle on this man's eyes, and laid his hands on him. Why do you think he didn't use the same "cookie cutter" approach for all his healings?

Other people brought the man to Jesus. This seems to be a pattern for many if not most of the miracles. Can you think of good reasons for getting more people involved in helping others? What are the benefits of working with others in your outreach ministry?

We all know someone who needs a helping hand. Can you think of one person God has put on your heart to befriend?

What does it mean to be a follower of Jesus—is it more than mind and theology? What does it look like on Main Street?

What are the practical implications of loving your brother as yourself?

In our world of scam artists and con men, what precautions are justified in serving others? Are these too daunting for your timid spirit?

Brainstorm how good people working together can serve our fellow man and still use sensible safety guides to protect ourselves.

HOMETOWN MIRACLES

When Jesus returned to his hometown and began teaching and healing, what were people's first reactions? (Amazement? Where did he get all this wisdom and miraculous powers?)

What changed their minds and caused them to take offense at him? (Gossip, jealousy, cynicism, disbelief?)

"He could not do any miracles there, except lay his hands on a few sick people and heal them. And he was amazed at their lack of faith." (Mark 6:5-6) Discuss the role of faith in qualifying one for a miracle—is it optional, desirable, or critical? Explain your conclusion.

How does your hometown respond when one of your own achieves great fame or fortune?

When have you encountered hostility, envy, disbelief, or competitive comparisons when you least expected them?

How can we avoid falling into such a trap of small-heartedness?

How can we grow into more mature Christians, sincerely rejoicing with others and applauding their successes?

AFTER JOHN'S BEHEADING

John the Baptist confronted King Herod, who had taken his brother's wife Herodias, telling him, "It is not lawful for you to have your brother's wife." Was this true? Was it wise, bold, or foolish for John to challenge Herod? Was John speaking politically or spiritually?

So Herodias nursed a grudge against God's prophet and wanted the king to have him killed. Was the Baptist's fiery preaching to the king an affront worthy of death? Why or why not? What are the dangers of harboring a grudge against someone who has angered you? How might this disagreement have been resolved peacefully? Have you ever held a grudge against anyone? How did you overcome the temptation to get even?

Herod wanted to kill John but knew him to be a righteous and holy man—and he feared his connection to God. He also liked to listen to John though some of his preaching puzzled him. Why then did King Herod let himself be beguiled and pressured into ordering John's murder?

Do you think the king consumed alcoholic beverages at his birthday banquet—and would that have affected his judgment?

Do you think the Holy Spirit used this tragic event to convince people to believe John's message of preparing their hearts for the arrival of Messiah? Had he finished his work as did Jesus? Explain your conclusion.

What practical life lessons do you find in this story?

When Jesus heard what happened to his beloved cousin, he withdrew by boat to a solitary place. Hearing of this, the crowds followed him on foot from the towns. When Jesus landed and saw the large crowd, he had compassion on them because they were like sheep without a shepherd. So he began teach them many things and healed their sick. What do you learn from this tender story about Jesus' aborted attempt to get away and grieve? How is it possible to lay aside your personal needs to help those without a shepherd?

JESUS COMES TO GENNESARET

They crossed the Sea of Galilee again, landing at Gennesaret. Soon people were rushing around, telling everyone to bring their sick to be cured. The sick ones begged Jesus to let them touch even his robe and all who did so were healed. The idea of Jesus being accessible, meeting us at our point of need, do you find this concept still valid? Explain your conclusion. Have you found the Lord approachable and accessible in your life? Elaborate.

People were rushing around to get word out that Jesus was in town; others were bringing people to him; still others were preparing places in the markets to lay sick people where Jesus would be passing by. If you believe you have a role in God's kingdom work, where are you along the path of discovery?

What are some of the service needs you see around you that seem to fit your talents and interests?

Where have you felt yourself being "stretched' to help someone in places or situations you didn't intentionally choose?

We see people in this story being healed by merely touching Jesus. Do you think this type of healing ministry is still going on? Have you seen it or been a part of such an outreach?

Faith opens a door to miracles; yet some of strong faith like Joni Erickson Tada have believed and prayed for a healing that did not come. Have you known such a case? How would you explain it to an unbeliever? (Joni is still paralyzed, yet she daily gives powerful testimonies of how God uses her in miraculous ways she could not have imagined.)

What do you think were the long-term impacts of the Lord's trip to Gennesaret? What practical insights do you take from this story?

A BLIND AND MUTE MAN

When Jesus restored this demon possessed man's sight and speech, the religious scalawags claimed, "It's only by Beelzebub that this fellow drives out demons." His own family said, "He's out of his mind!" When have you been misunderstood, maligned, or falsely accused for doing a good thing? What happened and was it worth taking the risk?

How did Jesus respond to jealousy, envy, suspicion, and character assignation? What insights do you gain from studying his delicate dance with wolves?

Jesus sensed the evil lurking in the Pharisees' hearts— literally read their minds. He used parables to expose and condemn them. How do you feel about the fact that Jesus knows what you're thinking, knows your motives, and what you are going to say and do? Do you fear it or welcome it and why? Does it help keep you accountable?

What are the dangers and rewards for refusing to let your enemies or detractors dictate your actions? What gives you courage to ignore them and do the right thing?

"This is war, and there is no neutral ground. If you're not on my side, you're the enemy; if you're not helping, you're making matters worse. If you're not gathering, you're scattering," Jesus told his audience— with his future killers listening. (Matthew 12:30 paraphrased) What does this mean for good people who hear the gospel but are still undecided about the claims of Christ? What did he mean by his comment about gathering and scattering?

"So I tell you that every sin and blasphemy can be forgiven—except blasphemy against the Holy Spirit, which will never be forgiven. Anyone who speaks against the Son of Man can be forgiven, but anyone who speaks against the Holy Spirit will never be forgiven, either in this world or in the world to come," Jesus warned them. (Matthew 12:31 NLT) Some say that rejecting Jesus as the Messiah is the only unpardonable sin. Do you agree or disagree—and why? Was Jesus saying the Pharisees committed the unpardonable sin by crediting to Satan this healing Jesus did by the power of the Holy Spirit? Explain your conclusion.

Have you ever wondered if you've committed the unpardonable sin? How did you resolve your concern? (Discuss with your group the following idea: As a believer, you don't need to worry about committing the unpardonable sin. You've believed in the One God sent to redeem you, you've been born again, the old person is dead, and you're alive forevermore.)

A SEVERED EAR RESTORED

"The one I kiss is the man you're after; arrest him," Judas told the crowd armed with swords and clubs, sent by the chief priests, lawyers, and elders to take Jesus by force. Going at once to Jesus, the betrayer said, "Greetings, Rabbi! At this prearranged signal, they seized Jesus and arrested him. Then Peter, who had a sword, drew it and struck the high priest's servant, cutting off his right ear. Jesus commanded Peter, "Put your sword away! Shall I not drink the cup the Father has given me?" When Peter chopped off the man's ear, he reacted in the heat of the moment. When has this been a problem for you? What is likely to set you off? How can your faith help you to stay calm?

Jesus rebuked Peter for resisting God's plan. Is this a common danger for believers? When have you been sorely tempted and how did you resolve it?

Jesus picked up the man's ear and restored it, powerfully demonstrating that love is God's way of overcoming all our enemies. Where are you on the road to loving your enemies? What is going to help you get where you need to be?

Jesus was soon to face treachery, mock trials, savage physical abuse, and crucifixion. Reflect with your group on those agonizing moments in the garden as he was praying—and how the Lord's response to these supreme crises could possibly help you face tomorrow.

"Pray that you will not fall into temptation," Jesus warned his disciples as they prepared for his death. The Lord knew they would run like rabbits when he was crucified—and afterward they would be hiding in terror and hunted as dangerous accomplices. The Lord knows what's in your future. How does knowing this help you—and how does his warning apply to you?

The disciples thought they were strong enough to stand firm but all of them failed miserably before being restored by the resurrected Lord. How strong do you think you are against your especially bothersome temptations? If you fail—or rather when you fail—how will you try to recover?

Then, all his disciples deserted him and fled. What is your first response to these sobering words? Every scripture is written for our edification, so how does this one edify you? What is most helpful to you in this story?

THE MIRACLE OF THE CROSS

"The Son of man will be crucified, but after three days in the grave, he will rise again." Jesus prepared his disciples for his approaching death and resurrection with words such as these. In this story, Jesus drove out crooked merchants and money-changers from the Temple. "What right have you to order them out?" the Jewish leaders asked. "If you have this authority from God, show us a miracle to prove it," they demanded. "All right," Jesus replied, "this is the miracle I will do for you: Destroy this temple (meaning his body) and in three days I will raise it up!" Question: when he fulfilled this promise on Easter morning, do you think they were convinced? Why or why not? From biblical accounts, discuss the reaction of the disciples, the religious blue bloods, and the people.

Is it easier or more challenging for people to accept the resurrection today than it was when it happened? Explain your conclusion.

Discuss the idea that embracing the cross and resurrection demands one's life be transformed. What does this look like in the public square? Who does the transforming? How big a deal is this for believers? For undecided or lukewarm observers?

The betrayal of Jesus by one of his beloved companions and trusted disciples is a sad reminder of human weakness and capacity for evil. How do your human failures, sins, and imperfections threaten to betray our Lord? What is your secret for overcoming them and living victoriously?

Chiseled in stone at the entrance to the Cemetery of the Pacific near Pearl Harbor are these sobering words: "What a costly sacrifice has been here laid on the altar of freedom." Discuss what the cross cost God our Father and Jesus his Son. What impact has it had on your life and future?

When Jesus first told his disciples he would die as a common criminal, their human reaction was predictable, "God forbid!" If you could look into your own future, would that be good or bad—and why? Discuss God's wisdom in not revealing your future to you today. If you were painting a canvas of God's dream for you, what would it look like—what would you want to capture in it? (Abundant life, joy, intimacy, fruitfulness, eternity?) If you had rejected God, how would your dream canvas look different?

The cross has been called the central event in human history. How would you describe it in your own words?

END OF STUDY GUIDE

NOTES FOR THE GROUP LEADER

Your role is key to the success of this group study. Almost any willing person can do it. Here are some helpful insights to guide you:

Be sure to prepare well before each session by studying the miracle story including relevant Bible passages, the study guide, and reflection questions.

Adults like to think for themselves and "own" the things they're learning. Thus, the best environment is one that encourages the group to reflect on the questions, share their insights, and allow others to do so.

As a leader of adults your role is to create a welcoming environment that encourages class members to explore and discover key spiritual concepts for themselves. This differs markedly from teaching children where the leader needs to be more pro-active in guiding students to the "right answers."

Your group will respond more favorably if you're open and transparent with them. Emphasize that you consider yourself to be a fellow student, learning and growing in how to live out your Christian faith every day—and are inviting them to partner with you on this exciting adventure.

See yourself as their guide and facilitator—not their teacher or lecturer. As their catalyst, you will be posing the discussion questions, and leading the group in creative sharing.

Once a question has been presented, relax and allow the group time to process it and respond. Resist the temptation to jump in before they've had opportunity to work it out themselves.

Be alert to prevent one person from dominating your discussions. In your first session, stress that we want everyone who wishes to have an opportunity to share their insights. Then, be prepared to step in and ensure this happens. If it becomes necessary, call on persons by name to give quieter members equal opportunity. (Some people may not be comfortable at first to share their thoughts. Make sure they know they can choose to pass if they prefer.)

Remember, you're helping one another grow in faith and applying these spiritual principles in your everyday lives. Keep in mind that developing lasting friendships and bonds of fellowship is a vital part of your ministry—possibly even more meaningful than the specific "lesson being covered." Thus, it is critical that you create a welcoming environment that helps people get to know and trust one another.

Begin each meeting by praying together. As you get to know one another, pray for any special concerns members are dealing with—and encourage one another to share special prayer concerns.

A key scriptural promise is that the Holy Spirit is given to lead us into all truth. Be sure to pray for the Holy Spirit's help as you study and prepare for each session.

When you distribute the book and study guide to the group, set the time and place for each meeting; tell them if you will be covering one miracle each session; and ask that they read and study the lesson to be covered and come prepared to participate.

Promise to begin each class promptly and end on time. Ask members to commit themselves to showing up on time. This is a matter of courtesy to one another since it minimizes disruptions and prevents the group from having to repeat what has already been covered.

As you lead the group thorough the suggested questions, ask if other thoughts or questions occurred to them as they studied the miracle story. Invite the group to respond by sharing their thoughts.

If the group is struggling with a particular question, you might draw them out by asking if anyone would share a personal experience that deals with this issue—and be prepared to step in with your own insights as needed.

Be sensitive to any special concerns you become aware of that are bothering any member of your group. Ask them privately if you can pray with them—and as a brother or sister in Christ offer to help them in any way you feel led by the Spirit. This includes helping them find professional counseling if appropriate.

Of God, Rattlesnakes, and Okra;
A Preacher's Boy Tells His Growing-Up Story

by J. Bennett Easterling

A heaping slice of old-fashioned Southern storytelling, this book gives readers a taste of genuine American life that will keep them coming back for more. Join the journey as a preacher's kid survives his father's stern discipline, rattlesnakes, and harvesting okra. The deep-fried characters are unforgettable, and the furry and feathered folks will steal the heart of animal lovers. Soaked in faith, people survived the lean, mean times, thanks to the velvet hearts they carried under their calluses, hard work, the good sense to laugh at themselves, and, often, the hand of God. What a delightful legacy they left us! Once you pick up this book, you'll be pleading, "Don't stop now and don't ever grow up!"

Endorsements:

"A warm, rich and interesting set of stories told through the eyes of a young preacher's son growing up on a farm." (Cutler)

"An absolutely captivating compilation of stories as told by a young preachers son living in the rural South in the early 20th Century." (Hust)

"I love this book and the author." (Love)

"Awesome book about a time that has passed but we can learn a lot from!" (kykimba)

"This book took me home." (Blankenship)

"Read it! You won't regret it." (Achey)

"Must read!" (Harrison)

What People Are Saying about Jesus Is Still Passing By

Jesus is Still Passing By is a wonderful, helpful overview of the miracles in a devotional form. Bennett highlights each miracle, adding helpful insights and present-day applications, allowing us to relate in a personal way to how *Jesus is Still Passing By*! Get this book and get lost in the wonder of Jesus, His miracles and His love for you!

Rev. Dennis W. Stueve
President, Lutheran Braille Works

The miracle stories we've loved since childhood never grow old, and sound even more alive in this new format that's more relevant to today's generation.

Kekeletso Lowe
Montgomery College Staff

In *Jesus Is Still Passing By*, our friend draws on his life-long relationship with the Lord Jesus. Reading these devotions is like sitting down with a godly grandfather who wants to impart the nuggets he's learned along the way. Using the miracles of Jesus, he offers insightful applications of God's unchanging truth to our lives today and reminds us His ways are still the best.

Jimmy & Hulda Bennett
Missionaries to Czechia

Ben has a real gift in the way he gives us insightful and relevant applications from the great miracles of Jesus. A treat to read.

Rondall Jones, Author, *Basic Readings in the New Testament*

What a refreshing read of our Jesus passing by over 2000 years ago and coming to life for us again today. Mr. Easterling's real-life stories give the miracles new life and made a renewed believer in me that miracles still happen. I'm compelled and highly encouraged by this book to find my miracle today!

Rachinee Pugh
Baptism Coordinator, Church of
the Redeemer, Gaithersburg MD

Jesus is Still Passing By engaged me as soon as I started reading. The devotions are easy to read and a blend of humor, storytelling, and Biblical teaching. The first devotion on the miracle at Cana immediately spoke to me and a situation I'm going through. I've found a new devotional guide!

David Pugh
Christian School Teacher

Do miracles still happen today? Are they relevant? I say yes! This book looks closely at the miracles of Jesus and what they mean to us, including examples of how God continues to work in our lives today. I was blessed, encouraged, and challenged to be a faithful witness of God's miracles in my life.

Amy Freese
Career Missionary
Guinea, West Africa

I found this delightful book to be well organized and easy to read. Bennett challenges you to take these stories and apply them to your own life— to reach out and treat others who have problems, as you would your own family. In helping others, he says you can offer them hope and love, encouraging them to also follow HIS teachings.

Bonnie Mayhew
Freelance Artist

A refreshingly frank and often humorous take on the NT miracles. This devotional does the bottom line well, getting to the punchline of prayerful reflections quickly. It's smooth - feels like I am listening to a warm and fuzzy friend feeding me bits and morsels of wisdom over a cup of coffee!

Vivian Farley
Christian Speaker, Leader, Moms in Prayer International

This book plumbs the depths of Jesus' miracles. By weaving the miracles with true stories from today and touches of humor, the narrative comes alive. Indeed, each miracle contains buried treasure which when discovered and applied produces radical life transformation. We're challenged and inspired to enter into a life God has always desired for us.

Chris Vennetti
Co-Founder, Disciple Nations International

LETTER TO THE READER

Dear Friend,

I hope you've enjoyed journeying back into the miracles, that you're challenged by the Reflection questions, and that you are inspired anew by these wonderful stories of God reaching down and touching people today. Our Savior is truly a Lord of miracles. Our every heartbeat testifies to his miraculous keeping power and his atonement for our salvation. How miraculous is that? Then, sending his Holy Spirit to live in us, he gives us a tiny part of his Kingdom work. How marvelous!

Now before you put down this book, may I ask for your help? Getting the word out about books is very important to any author. Would you be willing to help?

The best way to help is to write a review of this book. You can leave the review on Amazon, Barnes & Noble, or other online bookseller's site. Or on Twitter, Instagram, Facebook, etc. Or you can share it with the publisher of this book. (Endorsements are also welcome—please send those to the publisher, too.)

If you are a blogger and like my book, a review on your blog will really help. My publisher can provide you with a graphic of the cover if you need that. (Or, if you would like to interview me for your blog, I would be happy to accommodate any interview request. Just contact me through my editor, editor@msipress.com).

Thank you for helping me get the word out that Jesus is still passing by,

J. Bennett Easterling

CPSIA information can be obtained
at www.ICGtesting.com
Printed in the USA
FFHW012259100219
50481482-55725FF